Integrating Microsoft
Office 97
Illustrated Brief Edition

David Beskeen
Elizabeth Eisner Reding

COURSE
TECHNOLOGY

ONE MAIN STREET, CAMBRIDGE, MA 02142

an International Thomson Publishing company I(T)P®

Cambridge • Albany • Bonn • Boston • Cincinnati • London • Madrid • Melbourne • Mexico City
New York • Paris • San Francisco • Singapore • Tokyo • Toronto • Washington

Integrating Microsoft Office 97—Illustrated Brief Edition

is published by Course Technology

Managing Editor:	Nicole Jones Pinard
Product Manager:	Jeanne Herring
Production Editor:	Nancy Ray
Developmental Editor:	Katherine T. Pinard, Ann Marie Buconjic
Composition House:	GEX, Inc.
QA Manuscript Reviewers:	John McCarthy, Brian McCooey, Greg Bigelow
Text Designer:	Joseph Lee
Cover Designer:	Joseph Lee

© 1997 by Course Technology — I(T)P®

For more information contact:

Course Technology
One Main Street
Cambridge, MA 02142

International Thomson Publishing Europe
Berkshire House 168-173
High Holborn
London WC1V 7AA
England

Thomas Nelson Australia
102 Dodds Street
South Melbourne, 3205
Victoria, Australia

Nelson Canada
1120 Birchmount Road
Scarborough, Ontario
Canada M1K 5G4

International Thomson Editores
Campos Eliseos 385, Piso 7
Col. Polanco
11560 Mexico D.F. Mexico

International Thomson Publishing GmbH
Königswinterer Strasse 418
53277 Bonn
Germany

International Thomson Publishing Asia
211 Henderson Road
#05-10 Henderson Building
Singapore 0315

International Thomson Publishing Japan
Hirakawacho Kyowa Building, 3F
2-2-1 Hirakawacho
Chiyoda-ku, Tokyo 102
Japan

Trademarks

Course Technology and the Open Book logo are registered trademarks of Course Technology. Illustrated Projects and the Illustrated Series are trademarks of Course Technology.

I(T)P® The ITP logo is a registered trademark of International Thomson Publishing Inc.

Some of the product names and company names used in this book have been used for identification purposes only and may be trademarks or registered trademarks of their respective manufacturers and sellers.

Disclaimer

Course Technology reserves the right to revise this publication and make changes from time to time in its content without notice.

ISBN 0-7600-4711-1

Printed in the United States of America

10 9 8 7 6 5 4 3 2

From the
Illustrated Series™ Team

At Course Technology we believe that technology will transform the way that people teach and learn. We are very excited about bringing you, instructors and students, the most practical and affordable technology-related products available.

▶ The Development Process

Our development process is unparalleled in the educational publishing industry. Every product we create goes through an exacting process of design, development, review, and testing.

Reviewers give us direction and insight that shape our manuscripts and bring them up to the latest standards. Every manuscript is quality tested. Students whose backgrounds match the intended audience work through every keystroke, carefully checking for clarity and pointing out errors in logic and sequence. Together with our own technical reviewers, these testers help us ensure that everything that carries our name is as error-free and easy to use as possible.

▶ The Products

We show both how and why technology is critical to solving problems in the classroom and in whatever field you choose to teach or pursue. Our time-tested, step-by-step instructions provide unparalleled clarity. Examples and applications are chosen and crafted to motivate students.

▶ The Illustrated Series™ Team

The Illustrated Series™ Team is committed to providing you with the most visual introduction to microcomputer applications. No other series of books will get you up to speed faster in today's changing software environment. This book will suit your needs because it was delivered quickly, efficiently, and affordably. In every aspect of business, we rely on a commitment to quality and the use of technology. Each member of the Illustrated Series™ Team contributes to this process. The names of all our team members are listed below.

The Team

Cynthia Anderson	Mary-Terese Cozzola	Jeanne Herring	Elizabeth Eisner Reding
Chia-Ling Barker	Carol Cram	Meta Chaya Hirschl	Art Rotberg
Donald Barker	Kim T. M. Crowley	Jane Hosie-Bounar	Neil Salkind
Ann Barron	Catherine DiMassa	Steven Johnson	Gregory Schultz
David Beskeen	Stan Dobrawa	Bill Lisowski	Ann Shaffer
Ann Marie Buconjic	Shelley Dyer	Chet Lyskawa	Dan Swanson
Rachel Bunin	Linda Eriksen	Kristine O'Brien	Marie Swanson
Joan Carey	Jessica Evans	Tara O'Keefe	Jennifer Thompson
Patrick Carey	Lisa Friedrichsen	Harry Phillips	Sasha Vodnik
Sheralyn Carroll	Jeff Goding	Nicole Jones Pinard	Jan Weingarten
Brad Conlin	Michael Halvorson	Katherine T. Pinard	Christie Williams
Pam Conrad	Jamie Harper	Kevin Proot	Janet Wilson

Preface

Welcome to *Integrating Microsoft Office 97 — Illustrated Brief Edition*! This book in our highly visual new design offers users of Microsoft Office 97 Professional a hands-on introduction to the integration features of the suite and also serves as an excellent reference for future use.

► Organization and Coverage

This text contains seven units that cover basic through advanced integration skills. In these units students learn how to work with the programs together by copying and pasting, linking, and embedding files from one program to another.

► About this Approach

What makes the Illustrated approach so effective at teaching software skills? It's quite simple. Each skill is presented on two facing pages, with the step-by-step instructions on the left page, and large screen illustrations on the right. Students can focus on a single skill without having to turn the page. This unique design makes information extremely accessible and easy to absorb, and provides a great reference for after the course is over. This hands-on approach also makes it ideal for both self-paced or instructor-led classes. The modular structure of the book also allows for great flexibility; you can cover the units in any order you choose.

Each lesson, or "information display," contains the following elements:

This icon indicates a CourseHelp 97 slide show is available for this lesson. See the Instructor's Resource Kit page for more information.

Each 2-page spread focuses on a single skill.

Concise text that introduces the basic principles in the lesson and integrates the brief case study.

Excel 97

Changing Attributes and Alignment of Labels

Attributes are font styling features such as bold, italics, and underlining. You can apply bold, italics, and underlining from the Formatting toolbar or from the Font tab in the Format Cells dialog box. You can also change the alignment of text in cells. Left, right or center alignment can be applied from the Formatting toolbar, or from the Alignment tab in the Format Cells dialog box. See Table C-2 for a description of the available attribute and alignment buttons on the Formatting toolbar. Excel also has predefined worksheet formats to make formatting easier. ✎ Now that he has applied the appropriate fonts and font sizes to his worksheet labels, Evan wants to further enhance his worksheet's appearance by adding bold and underline formatting and centering some of the labels.

Steps

CourseHelp
The camera icon indicates there is a CourseHelp available with this lesson. Click the Start button, point to programs, point to CourseHelp, then click Word 97 Illustrated. Choose the CourseHelp that corresponds to this lesson.

QuickTip
Highlighting information on a worksheet can be useful, but overuse of any attribute can be distracting and make a document less readable. Be consistent by adding emphasis the same way throughout a workbook.

Time To
⌙ Save

1. Press [Ctrl][Home] to select cell A1, then click the Bold button **B** on the Formatting toolbar
The title "Advertising Expenses" appears in bold.

2. Select the range A3:J3, then click the Underline button **U** on the Formatting toolbar
Excel underlines the column headings in the selected range.

3. Click cell A3, click the Italics button **I** on the Formatting toolbar, then click **B**
The word "Type" appears in boldface, italic type. Notice that the Bold, Italics, and Underline buttons on the Formatting toolbar are indented. You decide you don't like the italic formatting. You remove it by clicking **I** again.

4. Click **I**
Excel removes italics from cell A3.

5. Add bold formatting to the rest of the labels in the range B3:J3
You want to center the title over the data.

6. Select the range A1:F1, then click the Merge and Center button **▦** on the Formatting toolbar
The title Advertising Expenses is centered across six columns. Now you center the column headings in their cells.

7. Select the range A3:J3 then click the Center button **▤** on the Formatting toolbar
You are satisfied with the formatting in the worksheet. Compare your screen to Figure C-8.

TABLE C-2: Attribute and Alignment buttons on the Formatting toolbar

icon	description	icon	description
B	Adds boldface	**▤**	Aligns left
I	Italicizes	**▤**	Aligns center
U	Underlines	**▤**	Aligns right
	Adds lines or borders	**▦**	Centers across columns, and combines two or more selected adjacent cells into one cell

► EX C-6 **FORMATTING A WORKSHEET**

Quickly accessible summaries of key terms, toolbar buttons, or keyboard alternatives connected with the lesson material. Students can refer easily to this information when working on their own projects at a later time.

Hints as well as trouble-shooting advice right where you need it — next to the step itself.

Clear step-by-step directions, with what students are to type in red, explain how to complete the specific task.

Every lesson features large, full-color representations of what the screen should look like as students complete the numbered steps.

The innovative design draws the students' eyes to important areas of the screens.

Brightly colored tabs above the program name indicate which section of the book you are in. Useful for finding your place within the book and for referencing information from the index.

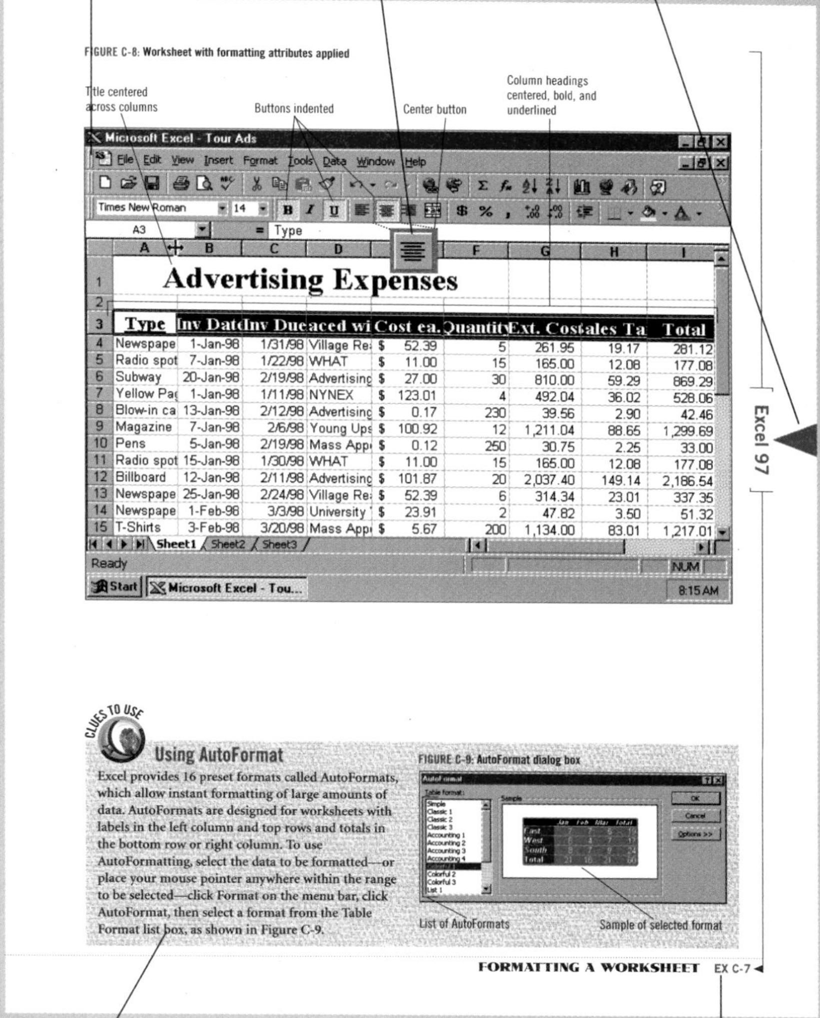

Other Features

The two-page lesson format featured in this book provides the new user with a powerful learning experience. Additionally, this book contains the following features:

▶ **Real-World Case**

The case study used throughout the textbook, a fictitious company called Nomad Ltd, is designed to be "real-world" in nature and introduces the kinds of activities that students will encounter when working with Microsoft Office 97. With a real-world case, the process of solving problems will be more meaningful to students.

▶ **End of Unit Material**

Each unit concludes with a Concepts Review that tests students' understanding of what they learned in the unit. A Skills Review follows the Concepts Review and provides students with additional hands-on practice of the skills they learned in the unit. The Skills Review is followed by Independent Challenges, which pose case problems for students to solve. At least one Independent Challenge in each unit asks students to use the World Wide Web to solve the problem as indicated by a Web Work icon. The Visual Workshops that follow the Independent Challenges help students to develop critical thinking skills. Students are shown completed documents and are asked to recreate them from scratch.

FIGURE C-8: Worksheet with formatting attributes applied

Title centered across columns

Buttons indented

Center button

Column headings centered, bold, and underlined

Excel 97

Using AutoFormat

Excel provides 16 preset formats called AutoFormats, which allow instant formatting of large amounts of data. AutoFormats are designed for worksheets with labels in the left column and top rows and totals in the bottom row or right column. To use AutoFormatting, select the data to be formatted—or place your mouse pointer anywhere within the range to be selected—click Format on the menu bar, click AutoFormat, then select a format from the Table Format list box, as shown in Figure C-9.

FIGURE C-9: AutoFormat dialog box

List of AutoFormats

Sample of selected format

FORMATTING A WORKSHEET EX C-7

Clues to Use Boxes provide concise information that either expands on the major lesson skill or describes an independent task that in some way relates to the major lesson skill.

The page numbers are designed like a road map. EX indicates the Excel section, C indicates Excel Unit C, and 7 indicates the page within the unit. This map allows for the greatest flexibility in content – each unit stands completely on its own.

Instructor's Resource Kit

The Instructor's Resource Kit is Course Technology's way of putting the resources and information needed to, teach and learn effectively into your hands. With an integrated array of teaching and learning tools that offer you and your students a broad range of instructional options, we believe this kit represents the highest quality and most cutting edge resources available to instructors today. Many of these resources are available online at www.course.com. The resources available with this book are:

CourseHelp 97 CourseHelp 97 is a student reinforcement tool offering online annotated tutorials that are accessible directly from the Start menu in Windows 95. These on-screen "slide shows" help students understand the most difficult concepts in a specific program. Students are encouraged to view a CourseHelp 97 slide show before completing that lesson. This text includes the following CourseHelp 97 slide shows:
• Using Object Linking and Embedding
Adopters of this text are granted the right to post the CourseHelp 97 files on any standalone computer or network.

Course Test Manager Designed by Course Technology, this cutting edge Windows-based testing software helps instructors design and administer tests and pre-tests. This full-featured program also has an online testing component that allows students to take tests at the computer and have their exams automatically graded.

Course Faculty Online Companion This new World Wide Web site offers Course Technology customers a password-protected Faculty Lounge where you can find everything you need to prepare for class. These periodically updated items include lesson plans, graphic files for the figures in the text, additional problems, updates and revisions to the text, links to other Web sites, and access to Student Disk files. This new site is an ongoing project and will continue to evolve throughout the semester. Contact your Customer Service Representative for the site address and password.

Course Student Online Companion This book features its own Online Companion where students can go to access Web sites that will help them complete the WebWork Independent Challenges. This page also contains links to other Course Technology student pages where students can find task references for each of the Microsoft Office 97 programs, a graphical glossary of terms found in the text, an archive of meaningful templates, software, hot tips, and Web links to other sites that contain pertinent information. These new sites are also ongoing projects and will continue to evolve throughout the semester.

Student Files To use this book students must have the Student Files. See the inside front or inside back cover for more information on the Student Files. Adopters of this text are granted the right to post the Student Files on any stand-alone computer or network.

Instructor's Manual This is quality assurance tested and includes:
• Solutions to all lessons and end-of-unit material
• Unit notes with teaching tips from the author
• Extra Independent Challenges
• Transparency Masters of key concepts
• Student Files
• CourseHelp 97

The Illustrated Family of Products

This book that you are holding fits in the Illustrated Series – one series of three in the Illustrated family of products. The other two series are the Illustrated Projects Series and the Illustrated Interactive Series. The Illustrated Projects Series is a supplemental series designed to reinforce the sills learned in any skills-based book through the creation of meaningful and engaging projects. The Illustrated Interactive Series is a line of computer-based training multimedia products that offer the novice user a quick and interactive learning experience. All three series are committed to providing you with the most visual and enriching instructional materials.

Contents

Office 97

Integration

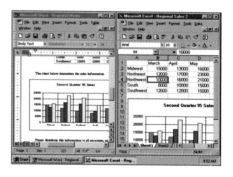

Integration

Contents

Integration

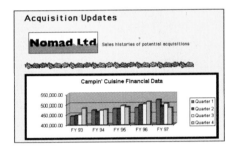

Integration

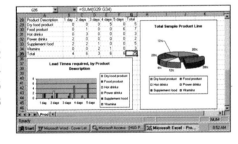

Integration

Integration

Introducing
Microsoft Office 97 Professional

Objectives

- ▶ **Understand Office 97 components**
- ▶ **Create documents with Word 97**
- ▶ **Build worksheets with Excel 97**
- ▶ **Manage data with Access 97**
- ▶ **Design presentations with PowerPoint 97**
- ▶ **Manage office tasks with Outlook**
- ▶ **Browse the World Wide Web with Internet Explorer 3**

Microsoft Office 97 Professional is a collection of programs designed to take advantage of the Windows 95 interface and improve your computer efficiency. When programs are grouped together, as in Microsoft Office, this collection is called a **suite**, and all its components have similar icons, functions, and commands. ✐ This unit will introduce you to Nomad Ltd, a tour and sporting goods company with five regional offices. Nomad Ltd organizes guided outdoor tours for activities like hiking, rafting, and biking. The company also sells the equipment needed to do these activities. By exploring how Nomad Ltd uses Microsoft Office components, you will learn how each program can be used in a business environment.

Understanding Office 97 Components

Microsoft Office contains all the programs commonly used in businesses. The documents created with Office programs can be opened without opening the program itself by using a button on the **Office Shortcut bar**. These buttons, listed in Table A-1, let you create new files, open existing files, use **Outlook**, a personal information manager, and travel the World Wide Web using Microsoft's web browser **Internet Explorer 3.0**. Since use of the Shortcut Bar is optional, it will not be covered in this book. The Microsoft Windows taskbar, located at the bottom of the screen, lets you switch between programs simply by clicking the program button. Office 97 is available in two arrangements: Professional and Standard. Office 97 Professional contains Access, the database program; Office 97 Standard does not. Nomad Ltd employees began using Office 97 Professional when the five regional offices switched from manual functions to networked personal computers. Figure A-1 is Nomad's organizational chart. Below are some of the ways the company uses Office 97 to create its Annual Report.

Create text documents using Word

Word is the word processor in Office. You use a **word processor** to create documents, such as descriptions of Nomad's financial condition and projected expansion reports.

Analyze sales figures using Excel

Excel is the spreadsheet in Office. You use a **spreadsheet** to analyze data and perform calculations. You can also use a spreadsheet to create charts to give a visual representation of the data.

Track product inventory using Access

Access is the database management system in Office. A **database** is a collection of related information like a list of employees and their social security numbers, salaries, and vacation time. A **database management system** organizes databases and allows you to cross-check information in them.

Create presentation graphics using PowerPoint

PowerPoint is the presentation graphics program in Office. You use **presentation graphics** to develop materials to enhance written reports and slides for visual presentations. Figure A-1 was created using PowerPoint.

Share or link text and graphics among programs to increase accuracy

Information in one program can be **dynamically linked** or **embedded** to another program. Using dynamic links or embedding techniques data in one file can be updated in other files. This means that an Excel chart linked to a PowerPoint slide will be automatically updated if a worksheet value changes. A company logo can be made available to all regional offices and placed in Word, Excel, Access, and PowerPoint files.

Schedule appointments, maintain a task list, record customer contact information with Outlook, and send electronic mail

This personal information manager has all the features of a hardcopy appointment book, and information can be shared with other Office programs. It's also a tool to send electronic mail.

Discover the ever-changing World Wide Web using Internet Explorer

The Internet Explorer lets you travel the World Wide Web, allowing you to access current information and global resources.

FIGURE A-1: Nomad Ltd organizational chart

Nomad Ltd

Headquarters
Boston, MA

Northeast	South	Midwest	Southwest	Northwest
Retail Outlets	Retail Outlets	Retail Outlets	Retail Outlets	Retail Outlets

CLUES TO USE

Understanding the docucentric environment

Office documents that were previously created can be opened using the Shortcut bar buttons or by clicking the filename in the Documents listing on the Start menu. This **docucentric** environment shifts the focus to completing document-related tasks rather than using the programs themselves.

TABLE A-1: Microsoft Office 97 Shortcut bar buttons

button	name	function
	Office	Add or remove Office programs and customize the Shortcut bar
	New Office Document	Create a document in any of the installed Office programs
	Open Office Document	Open a document in any of the installed Office programs
	New Message	Launch Microsoft Exchange, an electronic mail program
	New Appointment	Create any appointment using Outlook
	New Contact	Add a contact to the Outlook address book
	Create Microsoft Outlook Task	Add a task to the Outlook To Do list

Creating Documents with Word 97

All of Nomad's regional offices use Word while gathering data for the Annual Report. Word allows you to create and edit text documents, such as a newsletter or correspondence. Using Word, you can compose a document, then easily modify it. The result is a professional-looking document. The actual Annual Report is created using Word. Below are some of the benefits of using Word.

Details

Enter text quickly and easily

Word makes it easy to enter text, and then edit it later. Rather than having to retype a document, the text can be rearranged or revised.

Create error-free copy

You use Word's spell checker after you finish typing. It compares each word in a document to a built-in dictionary and notifies you if it does not recognize a word. Word's AutoCorrect feature automatically corrects words as you type them. Word provides several entries for commonly misspelled words, but you can add your own.

Combine text and graphics

Using Word, you can combine text and graphics easily. Figure A-2 shows the Word document containing text and graphics as it looks on the screen; Figure A-3 shows the completed sample memo.

Add special effects

Word gives you the ability to create columnar documents, drop caps (capital letters that take up two or three lines), and WordArt (text you customize by changing its appearance to become 3-dimensional or shadowed), adding a professional quality to your documents.

FIGURE A-2: Microsoft Word containing memo

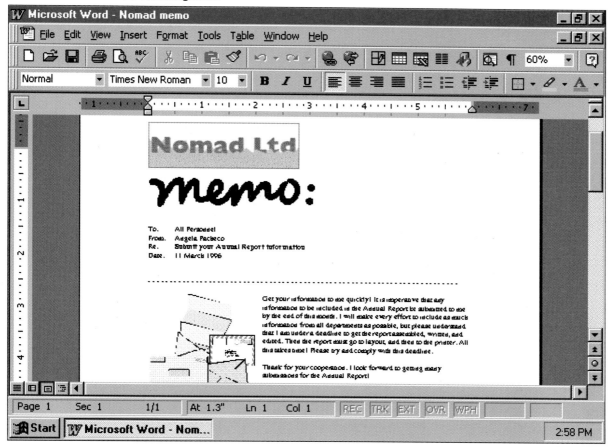

FIGURE A-3: Memo created in Word

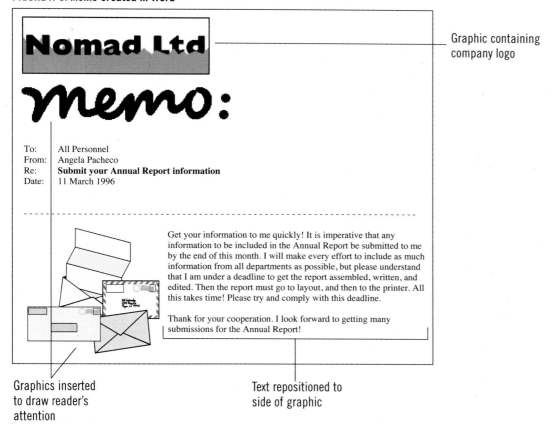

Graphic containing
company logo

Graphics inserted
to draw reader's
attention

Text repositioned to
side of graphic

Building Worksheets with Excel 97

The Excel program performs numeric calculations rapidly and accurately. Like traditional paper-based spreadsheets, an electronic spreadsheet contains a **worksheet** area that is divided into columns and rows which form individual **cells**. Cells can contain text, numbers, formulas, or a combination of all three. Sales and revenue data collected by Nomad's employees is stored and manipulated using Excel and then used in the Annual Report. What follows are some of the benefits of using Excel.

Details

 Calculate results quickly and accurately
Using Excel, you enter only data and formulas and then Excel calculates the results.

 Recalculate easily
Excel recalculates any results based on a changed entry automatically.

 Speculate outcomes using what-if analysis
Because equations are automatically recalculated, this lets you say "what-if" and create a variety of scenarios. For example, you could anticipate and avoid a revenue shortfall if expenses were to rise 15%.

 Complete complex mathematical equations
Using Excel's Paste Function, you can easily complete complicated math computations using built-in equations. The Paste Function tells you what data is needed and you fill-in-the-blanks. This saves you valuable time.

 Create charts
Excel makes it easy to create charts based on information in a worksheet. With Excel, charts are automatically updated as data changes. The worksheet in Figure A-4 shows a column chart that graphically shows the distribution of sales for each of Nomad's regional offices.

 Create attractive output
Printouts of numeric data can be made more attractive using charts, graphics, and text formatting such as bolding and italicizing, as shown in Figure A-5.

FIGURE A-4: Microsoft Excel containing worksheet

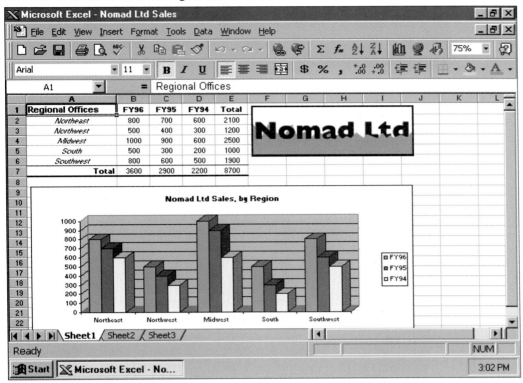

FIGURE A-5: Sales summary and chart created in Excel

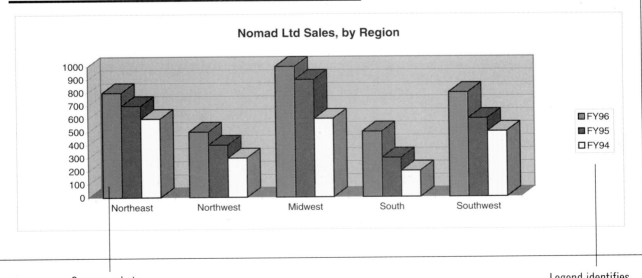

Sales Summary

Regional Offices	FY96	FY95	FY94	Total
Northeast	800	700	600	2100
Northwest	500	400	300	1200
Midwest	1000	900	600	2500
South	500	300	200	1000
Southwest	800	600	500	1900
Total	3600	2900	2200	8700

Corresponds to Northeast sales data for FY96

Legend identifies colors used in chart

Managing Data with Access 97

In addition to Word and Excel, Office 97 includes Access, a database manager. Access is used to arrange large amounts of data in various groups or **databases**, such as an inventory of products. The information in the databases can be retrieved in a variety of ways. For example, a database like an inventory list might be arranged alphabetically, by stocking location, or by the number of units on order. A powerful database, such as Access, lets you look up information quickly, easily, and in a wide variety of ways. ✐ Once the Annual Report is completed, the database containing stockholders names and address will be used to generate mailing labels so the report can be distributed. Below are some of the benefits of using Access.

Details

Enter data easily
Employees enter inventory items in whatever order they are received. Because Access organizes the data for you, the order in which items are entered is not a concern.

Retrieve data easily
Access makes it easy for you to specify criteria, or conditions, and then produce a list of all data that conforms to that criteria. You might want to see a list of products by supplier or a list of discontinued products. Figure A-6 shows a list of bicycle products sold at Nomad's retail stores sorted by product name then by the supplier ID number.

Create professional-looking forms
You can enter data into an on-screen form that you create in Access. This makes entering data more efficient, and you'll be less prone to making errors. Figure A-7 shows a screen form which can be used for data entry.

Add graphics to printed screen forms and reports
Forms and reports can contain graphic images, text formatting, and special effects, such as WordArt to make them look more professional. Beautifully designed screen forms can contain graphics and can be printed, as seen in Figure A-8.

FIGURE A-6: **List of bicycle inventory containing selected table files**

Product ID	Product Name	Supplier ID	Units In Stock	Unit Price
11162	Look PP166 pedals	94	45	$45.00
11162	Look PP166 pedals	91	45	$45.00
11162	Look PP166 pedals	63	45	$45.75
11162	Look PP166 pedals	63	45	$45.00
11162	Look PP166 pedals	63	45	$45.00
11162	Look PP166 pedals - adv	63	45	$45.00
11162	Look PP168 pedals	63	45	$45.00
76662	Nomad Aerospoke Wheels	56	30	$200.00
76662	Nomad Aerospoke Wheels	56	30	$200.00
76662	Nomad Aerospoke Wheels	56	30	$200.00
76662	Nomad Aerospoke Wheels	56	30	$200.00
76662	Nomad Aerospoke Wheels	56	30	$200.00
32323	Nomad Beauty Handlebar	10	27	$3.00
32323	Nomad Beauty Handlebar	10	27	$2.00

Items first sorted alphabetically by product name

Consecutive entry numbers rearranged by sort orders

Items then sorted in descending order by Supplier ID

FIGURE A-7: **Microsoft Access containing form**

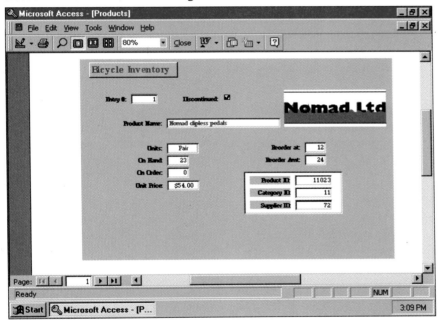

FIGURE A-8: **Inventory screen form created in Access**

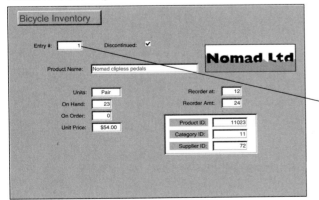

Field number automatically advances to the next number with each new entry

Designing Presentations Using PowerPoint 97

In PowerPoint, a **slide** is the work area in which handouts, outlines, speakers' notes and 35mm slides are produced. You can also create an online slide show in which flowing images appear on a PC monitor and are viewed by a group of people. Usually the computer is hooked up to a projector so a roomful of many people can see the demonstration.  The Annual Report is presented at the Annual Meeting using a variety of materials created in PowerPoint. The following are benefits of using PowerPoint.

Create and edit easily on a slide
Text can be written directly on a PowerPoint slide, enabling you to see if your slide looks cluttered. Editing is accomplished using the same methods as in Word. Text can be cut, copied, pasted, and moved simply and easily.

Combine information from Office 97 programs
Data created in Word, Excel, and Access can all be utilized in slides. This means that information created in Excel, for example, can be used on a slide, without having to be retyped.

Add graphics
Graphic images, such as clip art, an Excel chart, or a corporate logo, further enhance any presentation materials. PowerPoint accepts the most commonly available graphic file formats and comes with more than 1,000 clip art images. PowerPoint also allows you to create your own shapes and design your own text. Figure A-9 shows a slide containing an Excel chart.

Print a variety of presentation materials
In addition to being able to print out a slide, as seen in Figure A-10, you can also create many other types of printed materials. Speakers Notes—containing hints and reminders helpful to whomever delivers the presentation—are invaluable. Handouts for presentation attendees contain a reduced image of each slide and a place for handwritten notes.

Special effects
Add special effects, such as transitions from one slide to the next, text and graphics builds within slides, sounds and videos all serve to make your presentation look professional.

FIGURE A-9: Microsoft PowerPoint containing slide

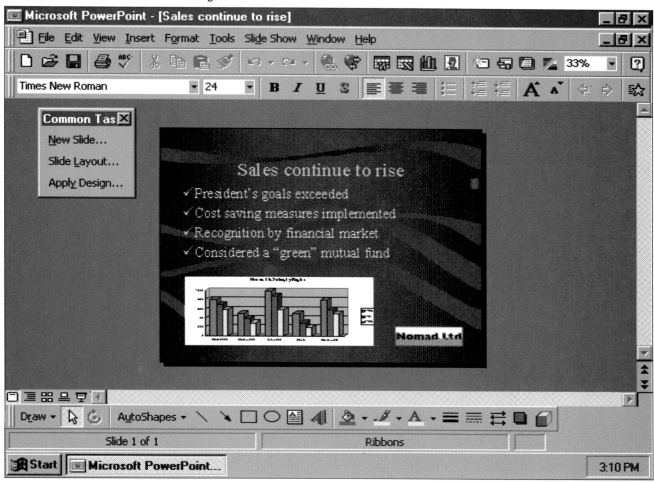

FIGURE A-10: Slide with Excel chart created in PowerPoint

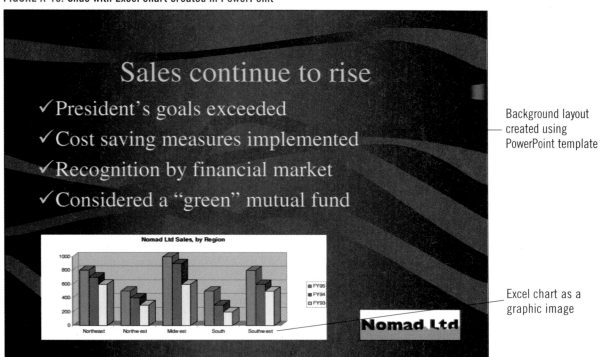

Background layout created using PowerPoint template

Excel chart as a graphic image

Managing Office 97 Tasks Using Outlook

There's more to office work than creating documents, worksheets, databases, and presentations. Outlook is a personal information manager that lets you better manage all the items that occur during a typical day. For example, you can send electronic mail—or **e-mail**—to anyone with an Internet address using the Inbox. <img> Nomad employees work more efficiently using Outlook to send messages, schedule appointments, and keep track of deadlines.

Details

 ### Process mail
Use the Inbox to read, forward, reply, and create e-mail. The Inbox, shown in Figure A-11, displays the first few lines of each unread message, so you can see if you want to read it now or wait until later. In addition to the actual content of a message, individual files can also be attached. This means you can send a colleague a document created in Excel, for example, along with an explanatory message.

 ### Create and maintain appointments
Just like an appointment that sits on your desk, Calendar lets you make appointments with others, plan meetings, and keep track of events such as seminars, hire dates, birthdays, and anniversaries. The task pad always displays, giving you an overview of items in your Task list.

 ### Manage tasks
Tasks lets you keep track of pending jobs, and allows you to set priorities that evaluate the relative importance of one job over another, assign due dates, and express completion expectations. You can also use the Task Request lets you assign a task to another person. This section allows you to monitor the relative status of the many tasks you manager.

 ### Keep track of business contacts
Its impossible to remember every persons name, address, and telephone number. Contacts lets you record vital information such as name, address, and phone number, but also includes space for e-mail addresses and web sites, as shown in Figure A-12.

 ### Maintain a journal
Outlook's Journal is a time management tool that lets you track project phases and record activities with ease. Icons of files related to specific activities can be embedded into the Journal so you'll always be able to return to them.

 ### Create reminders using Notes
Since it's difficult to remember all the things you have to do, use Notes—just like sticky yellow papers attached to items on folders—to leave messages for yourself. These electronic notes serve as reminders of important information that might otherwise get lost on your desk.

FIGURE A-11: Microsoft Outlook Inbox

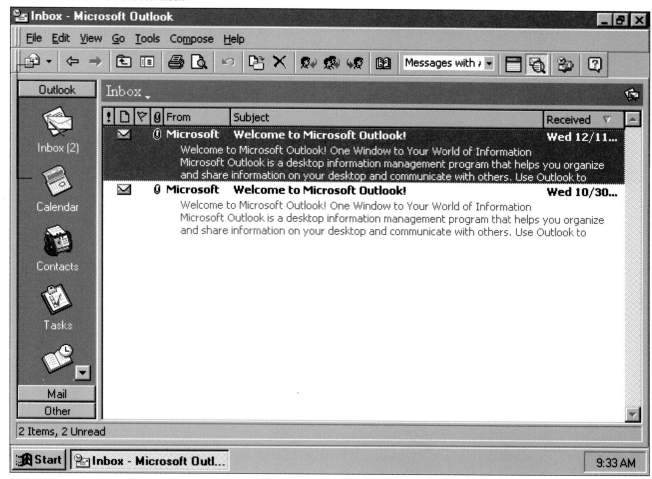

FIGURE A-12: Contact dialog box in Outlook

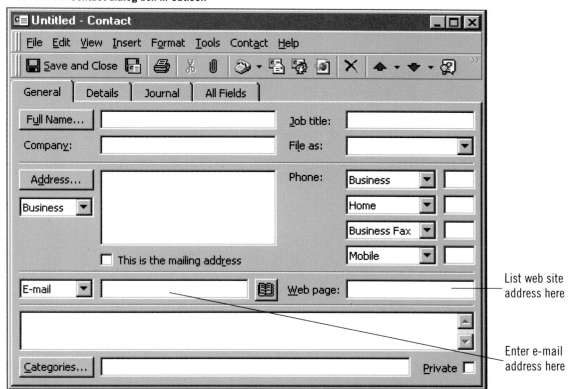

Browsing the World Wide Web with Internet Explorer 3

The World Wide Web—also know as the **Web**—is an element of the Internet that brings global information to your desktop in a graphical format. Internet Explorer 3 is a **browser**, software designed to view the graphic images and multimedia data on the Web. Many Web sites let you move to other sites with the click of your mouse using **links**, instructions that take you to different web site addresses. You can also quickly jump to Web sites entered in any Outlook's Contact. Nomad employees keep informed and up-to-date on the latest trends using Internet Explorer.

Details

 Display Web sites

Once you're connected to the Internet, you can view interesting and informative Web pages from all around the globe.

 Jump to a Web site listed in Contacts

If you've entered a web site in Contacts as shown in Figure A-13, you can quickly access that site by clicking that Contact, then clicking the Explore Web Page button.

 Move from one Web site to another

Links found within a Web page let you effortlessly move from site to site. This lets you easily find information related to the topic you're interested in.

 Save your favorite site locations

Once you've located interesting Web sites, you'll want to save their addresses so you can return to them. Internet Explorer makes it easy to compile a list of your favorite locations.

 Use multimedia

Video and audio clips are commonly found within Web pages, and you can take advantage of the depth they add by using a browser that's multimedia-capable, such as Internet Explorer.

 Print Web pages

As you travel the Web, you may want to print the information you find. You can easily print an active Web page—including text and graphics.

FIGURE A-13: Browsing with Internet Explorer

Practice

► Concepts Review

Label each of the elements in Figure A-14.

FIGURE A-14

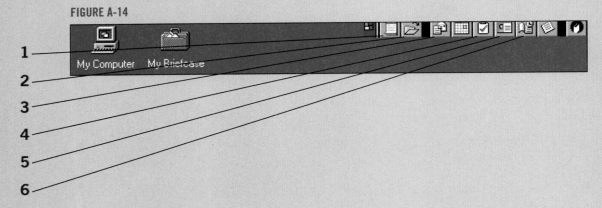

1
2
3
4
5
6

Match each program with the correct icon.

7. **Microsoft PowerPoint**   a.
8. **Microsoft Outlook**   b.
9. **Microsoft Excel**   c.
10. **Microsoft Word**   d.
11. **Microsoft Access**   e.

Select the best answer from the list of choices.

12. **Excel can be used for all of the following tasks, except:**
    a. Entering columns or rows of numbers
    b. Creating charts
    c. Creating columnar text
    d. Recalculating numeric data

13. **Which of the following is not a feature found in Word?**
    a. AutoCorrect
    b. Drop cap
    c. Slide
    d. Columnar documents

14. **Text in a Word document can:**
    a. Be easily modified and rearranged
    b. Contain graphics
    c. Be in a columnar format
    d. Contain all these effects

15. **You can create an on-line slide show containing graphics and text using:**
    a. Word
    b. PowerPoint
    c. Excel
    d. Access

16. **You can enter data easily in Access using:**
    a. Slides
    b. Charts
    c. On-screen forms
    d. Formulas

17. **PowerPoint can create all of the following, except:**
    a. Handouts
    b. Slides
    c. Outlines
    d. Data entry screen forms

Integrating
Word and Excel

Objectives

▶ **Open multiple programs**
▶ **Copy Word data into Excel**
▶ **Create a dynamic link (DDE) from Excel to Word**

Now that you have experienced the power of Word and Excel, it is time to learn how to integrate the programs. When you integrate programs, you combine information between them without retyping anything.

Andrew Gillespie, the national sales manager for Nomad Ltd, collected the spring quarter sales data for clothing from the five sales regions. He compiled this information in a Word document, and now he wants to add an Excel column chart to his document. Andrew will use simple integration techniques to do this. He will then give the data back to the regional managers so each manager can see how his or his own region compared to the other four regions.

Opening Multiple Programs

When you are integrating information from one program to another, it is helpful to have both files open at the same time. The Windows environment gives you the ability to have more than one program open at a time. This is sometimes called **multitasking**. Before integrating the data, Andrew starts both Word and Excel. To make integrating the data easier, he aligns each program window side by side on the screen.

1. Click the Start button on the taskbar, then point to Programs
   The Programs menu opens.

2. Click Microsoft Word in the Program list
   The Word program button appears in the taskbar. Minimize the program window.

3. Click the Minimize button in the program window
   The Word program window appears to shrink into the program button on the taskbar. Next, open the Excel program.

4. Click the Start button on the taskbar, point to Programs, then click Microsoft Excel
   A blank Excel workbook appears. You use the taskbar to maximize the Word program and make it active.

5. Click the Word program button on the taskbar
   Word maximizes and becomes the active program. Excel is still open, but it is not active, as shown in Figure A-1. Now, arrange the program windows so each occupies half of the screen.

6. Right-click the taskbar
   The taskbar pop-up menu appears.

7. Click Tile Vertically
   The two program windows each occupy half of the screen. Compare your screen to Figure A-2. The title bars of both windows are gray and both program buttons on the taskbar are raised indicating that neither program window is active.

FIGURE A-1: Word document active and Excel workbook inactive

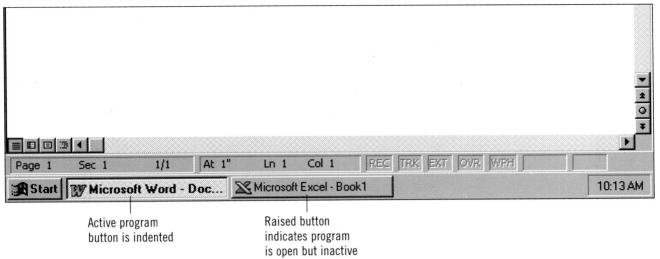

Active program
button is indented

Raised button
indicates program
is open but inactive

FIGURE A-2: Word window and Excel window on the screen

Each program
displays its own
toolbars

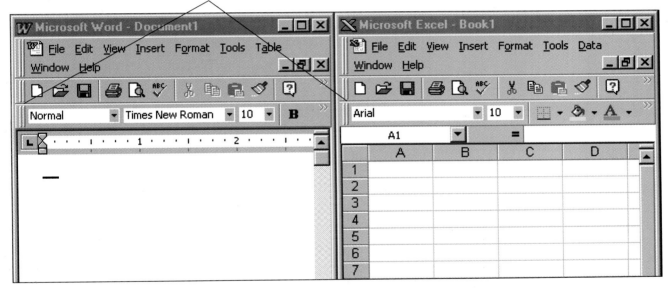

CLUES TO USE

Using shortcut keys to switch between open programs

You can switch between open programs by using the shortcut key combination [Alt][Tab]. Pressing [Alt][Tab] causes the icons and names of open programs (whether or not they are minimized) to appear in the center of the screen, as shown in Figure A-3. To see this on the screen, press and hold [Alt], then press and release [Tab]. If more than one program is open, press and release [Tab] again while still holding down [Alt] to move the selection box to the next icon in the center of the screen. When the program you want to activate is selected, release [Alt].

FIGURE A-3: Word program icon in the center of the Excel worksheet

Copying Word Data into Excel

Moving or copying information from one program to another is just like moving or copying information within a single program. You can use the program's Cut, Copy, and Paste commands, buttons on the toolbars, or the drag-and-drop method to move or copy information. Andrew typed a memo to the regional managers that includes a Word table containing the spring quarter sales data from all five regions. He wants to add a column chart to the memo. To create the column chart in Excel, Andrew needs to first copy the data into an Excel workbook.

Steps

1. **Click anywhere within the Word program window to make it active**
   Just like two windows open in the same program, clicking in a window makes that window active. Open your memo.

2. **Open the file INT A-1 from your Student Disk**
   Save this document on your Student Disk.

3. **Save this file as Regional Memo on your Student Disk**
   Regional Memo appears in the Word program window in Page Layout View. To make more of the document visible, reduce the percentage of the document's scale from 100% to 75%.

4. **Click View on the menu bar, click Zoom, click the 75% option button, then click OK**

5. **Scroll down until you can see the table and the body of the memo, then click the right scroll arrow once so you can see the entire table as shown in Figure A-4**
   The Word document is the **source file**—the file from which the information is copied. The Excel workbook is the **target file**—the file that receives the copied information. You will copy the table containing the spring quarter sales data.

6. **Position the pointer in the selection bar next to the top row of the table until the pointer changes to ⇗ , press and hold the mouse button to select the top row of the table, drag the pointer down until all of the rows are selected, then release the mouse button**

7. **Press and hold [Ctrl], click within the table so the pointer looks like ⇖ , drag the pointer to the Excel worksheet so the destination of the table's outline is in the range A1:D6, as shown in Figure A-5, then release the mouse button and [Ctrl]**
   The information in the Word table is copied into the Excel worksheet, as shown in Figure A-6. Using drag-and-drop is the easiest way to copy information from a source file to a target file.

8. **Click the Save button 🖫 on the Excel Standard toolbar, then save the workbook as Regional Sales 1 on your Student Disk**
   Now that the data is copied into the Excel worksheet, you can easily create the column chart for the memo.

9. **Close the Regional Sales 1 workbook file, but do not exit Excel**
   Do not close the Regional Memo Word file.

QuickTip
You also can select the Word table, click the Copy button on the Word Standard toolbar, then click the first destination cell in Excel and click the Paste button on the Excel Standard toolbar.

FIGURE A-4: Regional Memo open

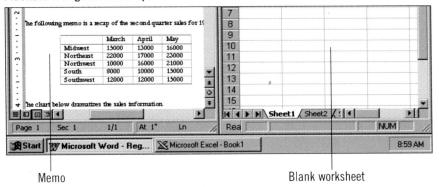

Memo   Blank worksheet

FIGURE A-5: Drag-and-drop Word text into an Excel worksheet

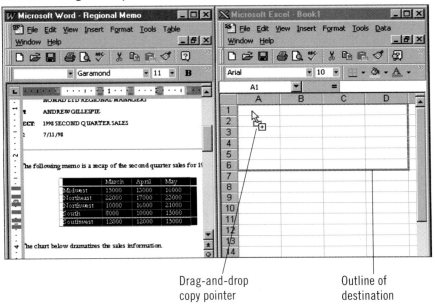

Drag-and-drop   Outline of
copy pointer   destination

FIGURE A-6: Word table data copied into an Excel worksheet

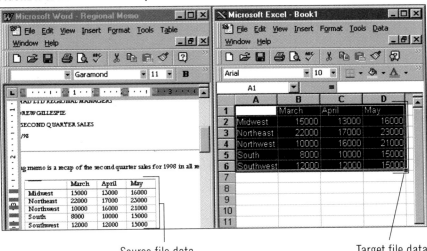

Source file data   Target file data

Integration

Creating a Dynamic Link (DDE) between Excel and Word

Sometimes you want the data in two programs to be dynamically linked, not just copied. A **dynamic link**—sometimes called **dynamic data exchange** or **DDE**—means that if the data in the source file is changed, the data in the target file will be automatically updated. Andrew created the column chart in Excel using the data that he had copied from the Word file. Now he wants to paste the chart into his memo. He decides to link it to the document rather than simply copy it, so that the Word memo will always reflect modifications made in the Excel worksheet.

1. In the Excel program window, open the file **INT A-2**, then save it as **Regional Sales 2**
   Regional Sales 2 appears in the Excel worksheet window, as shown in Figure A-7. This file contains the chart created using the data copied from the Word document. You want to copy the chart into the Word document using a dynamic link to the Excel worksheet.

QuickTip

If the Chart toolbar is in the way, drag it by its title bar to a new location.

2. Right-click the **chart** to select it and open the pop-up menu, then click **Copy** on the pop-up menu
   A moving, dotted selection box appears around the chart and the chart is copied to the Clipboard. Now, position the insertion point in the Word document where you want the chart to appear.

3. Click anywhere in the Word program window to make it active, click the **left scroll arrow** once, then click in the blank paragraph below the sentence that begins "The chart below dramatizes…"

4. Click **Edit** on the Word menu bar, click **Paste Special** to open the Paste Special dialog box, click the **Paste link option button**
   The As list box in the Paste Special dialog box changes to list the contents of the Clipboard.

5. Make sure **Microsoft Excel Chart Object** is listed in the As list box, then click **OK**
   The chart is copied into the Word document, and a dynamic link is created between the Word document and the Excel worksheet. Click the scroll buttons to make the chart more visible, if necessary. One of the sales figures is incorrect. The March sales for the Northeast were actually $12,000.

6. Make the Excel worksheet window active, then click cell **B3**

7. Type **12000** then press **[Enter]**
   Watch the chart as the second column, which depicts the Northeast data series, shrinks to reflect the new data. This change occurs in both the Excel worksheet and in the Word document, as shown in Figure A-8.

Time To
✔ Save
✔ Close
✔ Exit Excel

8. Make the Word window active if necessary, click the **Maximize button** in the program window, then click the **Save button** 🖫 on the Word Standard toolbar to save the document

9. Click the **Print Preview button** 🔍 on the Word Standard toolbar, examine your document, click the **Print button** 🖨 on the Print Preview toolbar, and finally close the document and exit Word

FIGURE A-7: Excel worksheet containing chart

Title bar of source document

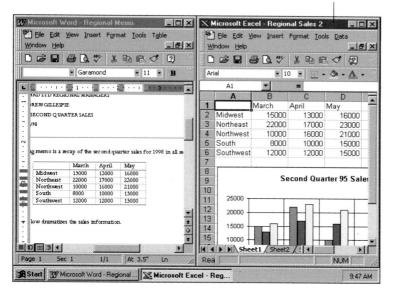

FIGURE A-8: Excel chart linked to Word document

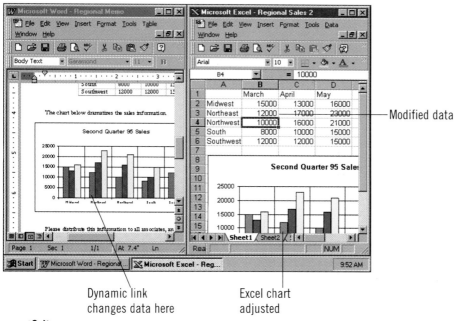

Modified data

Dynamic link changes data here

Excel chart adjusted

Breaking links

If you are working with a file containing linked data and you decide that you don't want the linked object to change if the source file changes, you can break the link. In other words, you can change the object from a linked object to a pasted object. In the target file, click the object to select it, click Edit on the menu bar, then click Links to open the Links dialog box, shown in Figure A-9. Click the name of the source file, click Break Link, then click OK. The object in the target file is no longer linked to the source file.

FIGURE A-9: Links dialog box

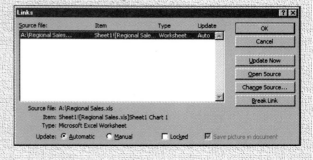

Practice

▶ Independent Challenges

1. The Chamber of Commerce realizes that to improve their advertising coverage, they need to hire an outside consultant. A list of promising consultants is being assembled by other Chamber members. Your job is to create a letter which gives them an overview of the Chamber's advertising efforts.

To complete this independent challenge:

1. Open the Excel file INT A-3 from your Student Disk and save it as Chamber Statistics. Open the Word file INT A-4 from your Student Disk and save it as Chamber Consultants.
2. Examine the chart in the Chamber Statistics workbook. Do you think you can use this chart within a document, or do you need to create other types of charts? What enhancements will need to be added to the charts?
3. Examine the Chamber Consultants file and determine what additions you will need to make to best inform the prospective consultant.
4. Update the date field code in the Chamber Consultants file to reflect the current date.
5. The letter to the Board should contain three charts. Create the additional charts you will need. Add any enhancements, such as text annotations and arrows, which you can call attention to in the letter.
6. Create the document text that will accompany each chart.
7. Paste the charts into the Word document.
8. Preview the Chamber Consultants file. When satisfied it is complete, save it, then print a copy.
9. Submit your printouts.

2. The US Census Bureau maintains a variety of current statistics on the World Wide Web. Using their web site, you can find population projections by state. Use the web site to find populations and projections and then create charts to explain the information.

To complete this independent challenge:

1. Use their web site to find information about state. Use the US Census Bureau's web site to compile your data.
2. Locate download and print the table that shows the Projections of the Total Population of States.
3. Open a new workbook and save it on your Student Disk as Population Projections.
4. Enter data for the United States for the years 1995, 2000, and 2005.
5. Create at least three charts of this data.
6. Open a new Word document and save it on your Student Disk as Population Analysis.
7. Write an description of each of the three Excel charts.
8. Link each of the charts to the Word document above each one's descriptive text.
9. Save, print and hand in print your work.

Integrating
Word, Excel, and Access

Objectives

► **Merge data between Access and Word**
► **Use Mail Merge to create a form letter**
► **Export an Access table to Excel**

You have learned how to use Word, Excel, and Access individually to accomplish specific tasks more efficiently. Now you will learn how to integrate files created using these programs so that you can use the best features of each one. ✎ In preparation for the upcoming Annual Report, Andrew Gillespie, the national sales manager for Nomad Ltd, wants to establish a tour customer profile that he can incorporate into the report. To do this, he will mail a survey to Nomad Ltd's tour customers. He also wants to export the Access database of customer names and addresses into an Excel worksheet so that he can create an Excel chart showing from which areas of the country Nomad attracts the most customers.

Integration

Merging Data Between Access and Word

Companies often keep a database of customer names and addresses, then send form letters to their customers. With Microsoft Office, you can combine, or **merge**, data from an existing Access table with a Word document to automatically create personalized form letters. Andrew wants to survey customers who have taken tours with Nomad during the last two years. He wrote a form letter using Word. He wants to merge his form letter with the customer names and addresses that already exist in an Access table.

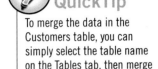

1. **Start Microsoft Access and open the file Customer Info from your Student Disk**
   The Database window for the file Customer Info opens. Open the Customers table.

QuickTip

To merge the data in the Customers table, you can simply select the table name on the Tables tab, then merge it with the Word document.

2. **Click the Tables tab if necessary, click Customers, then click Open**
   The Customers table is the **data source** for the Mail Merge. To merge the Customers table data with the survey form letter, use the Office Merge It feature.

3. **Click Tools on the menu bar, point to Office Links, then click Merge It with MS Word**
   The Microsoft Word Mail Merge Wizard dialog box appears, as shown in Figure B-1. The Mail Merge Wizard links your data to a Microsoft Word document. The customer survey form letter already exists as a Word document, so accept the default option to link your data to an existing Microsoft Word document.

4. **Click OK**
   The Select Microsoft Word Document dialog box opens.

Trouble?

If a message box appears telling you that there isn't enough memory to open the document file, exit all open programs and try launching Word prior to Step 1.

5. **Select the file INT B-1 from your Student Disk, then click Open**
   Word opens and the document INT B-1 appears in the document window below the Mail Merge toolbar. Table B-1 describes the buttons in the Mail Merge toolbar. The document you just opened is the **main document** for the Mail Merge.

6. **If the Word program window does not fill the screen, click the Word program window Maximize button**
   The Word program window resizes to fill the entire screen. See Figure B-2. Save the document with a new name.

7. **Click File on the menu bar, click Save As, then save the document as Survey Form Letter to your Student Disk**
   In the next lesson, you will continue setting up the mail merge.

TABLE B-1: Mail Merge buttons

name	button	name	button
≪≫ ABC	View Merged Data		Check for Errors
⏮	First Record		Merge to New Document
◀	Previous Record		Merge to Printer
1	Go to Record		Mail Merge
▶	Next Record		Find Record
⏭	Last Record		Edit Data Source
	Mail Merge Helper		

FIGURE B-1: Microsoft Mail Merge Wizard dialog box

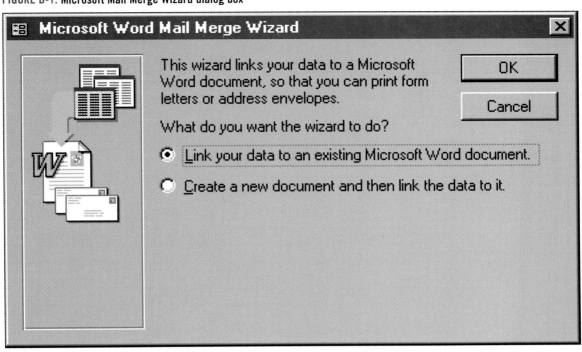

FIGURE B-2: Main document

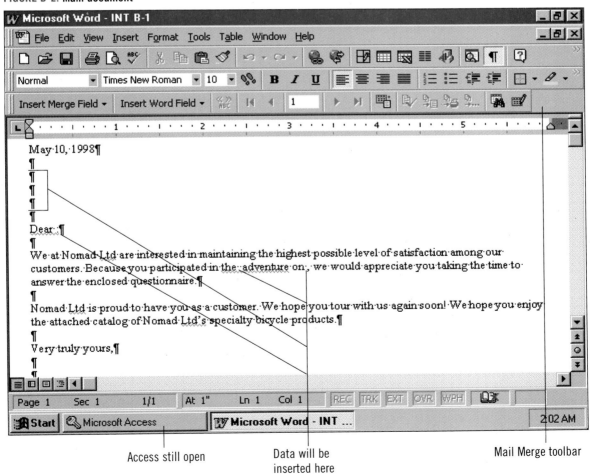

Access still open

Data will be
inserted here

Mail Merge toolbar

Using Mail Merge to Create a Form Letter

Once you have opened and linked the form letter and the Access table, you are ready to insert merge fields into the letter. When you perform the Mail Merge, Access looks for the merge fields in the main document and replaces them with the appropriate field from the data source. After opening the data source and selecting the main document, Andrew needs to insert merge fields into the main document.

Trouble?

If you can't see the paragraph symbols, click the Show/Hide ¶ button ¶ on the Standard toolbar.

1. Position the pointer in the second empty paragraph below the date, then click the **Insert Merge Field menu button** on the Mail Merge toolbar

A list of fields in the Access database appears, as shown in Figure B-3. The first merge field you need to insert is the FirstName field in the inside address.

2. Click **FirstName**

The FirstName field is inserted between brackets in the form letter.

3. Press [Spacebar], click the **Insert Merge Field menu button** on the Mail Merge toolbar, click **LastName**, then press [↓]

4. Continue inserting the merge fields and typing the text shown in Figure B-4

Make sure you insert a comma and a space after the City merge field and a space after the State merge field. After all the merge fields are entered, save the main document.

5. Click the **Save button** 🖫 on the Standard toolbar

Before you merge the data, make sure the merged data appears correctly in the main document.

6. Click the **View Merged Data button** ⟨⟨»⟩ on the Mail Merge toolbar

The data from the first record (Ginny Braithwaite) appears in the main document as shown in Figure B-5. There are several ways to merge the main document with the data source. If you want to merge the main document with records that meet certain criteria, click the Mail Merge button on the Mail Merge toolbar, then set query options. If you want to merge the files directly to the printer, click the Merge to Printer button on the Mail Merge toolbar. It's a good idea to merge the documents into one new document so that you can examine the final product and make any necessary corrections before you print. Do this now.

7. Click the **Merge to New Document button** 🖫 on the Mail Merge toolbar

"Microsoft Word – Form Letters1" appears in the title bar. You should see the first form letter with Ginny Braithwaite's data on your screen. Save the merged document before printing.

8. Click 🖫 on the Standard toolbar, then save the document as **Survey Letters** to your Student Disk

Now print the document.

9. Click **File** on the menu bar, click **Print**, specify pages 1 through 3 to print only the first three form letters, then click **OK**

The first three of the 30 form letters print. Now exit Word.

10. Click **File** on the menu bar, click **Exit**, then click **No** to save changes to Survey Form Letter

Word closes and returns you to Access.

FIGURE B-3: List of fields in Access database

Fields in data source

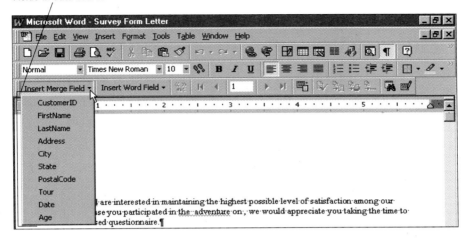

FIGURE B-4: Main document with merge fields inserted

Inserted merge fields

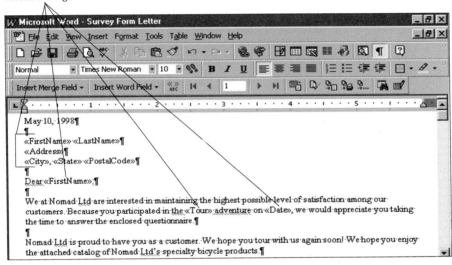

FIGURE B-5: Main document with merged data

Fields from first
record in data source

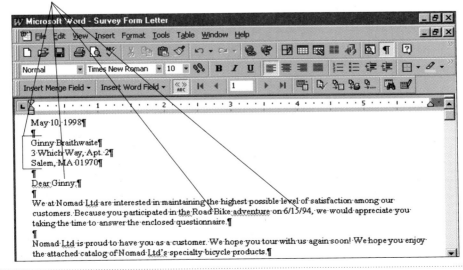

Integration

Exporting an Access Table to Excel

Data in an Access table can be exported to Excel and several other applications. When a table is exported, a copy of the data is created in a format acceptable to the other application, and the original data remains intact.　　　Andrew wants to export the Customer's table in the Customer Info database into Excel so that he can analyze the data. Later he will create a chart that shows the distribution of Nomad's customers by tour type.

Steps

1. Make sure the Customers table is active

2. Click **Tools** on the menu bar, point to **Office Links,** then click **Analyze It with MS Excel**
   The exported data appears in an Excel workbook named Customers that contains only one worksheet, also named Customers. When data is imported into Excel, only one worksheet is supplied, although more can be added. First, maximize the Excel program window if it is not already maximized.

3. If necessary, click the Excel program window **Maximize button**
   Resize the columns so that you can see all the data

4. Select the **A through J column selector buttons,** click **Format** on the menu bar, point to **Column,** click **AutoFit Selection,** then press **[Home]** to return to cell A1
   The column widths resize to fit the data in the worksheet. Sort the table so you can look up customer information faster.

5. Click **Data** on the menu bar, then click **Sort**
   The Sort dialog box appears, as shown in Figure B-6. Notice that the header row option button is selected. This means that the first row in the worksheet will not be sorted. Sort the table by state and then by last name.

6. Click the **list arrow** in the Sort by section, click the **down scroll arrow,** click **State,** click the **list arrow** in the Then by section, click **Last Name,** then click **OK**
   Compare your screen to Figure B-7. Now save and print the worksheet.

7. Click the **Save button** 🖫 on the Standard toolbar, then click the **Print button** 🖨 on the Standard toolbar

8. Click **File** on the menu bar, click **Exit** to exit Excel, then in the Access program window, click **File** on the menu bar and click **Exit** to exit Access

Trouble?

If a message appears telling you that the workbook was created in a previous version of Excel, click yes to update it.

FIGURE B-6: Sort dialog box

Sort on State first   Sort on Last Name second

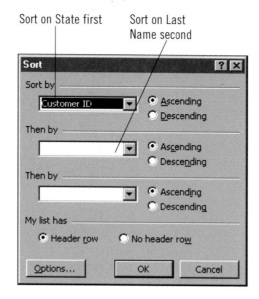

FIGURE B-7: Excel worksheet with sorted data

Sorted on last name second   Sorted on state first

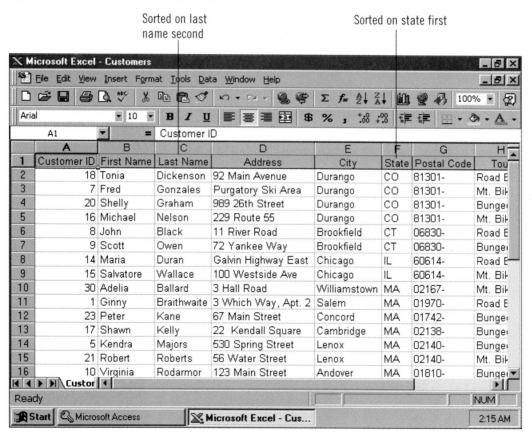

Exporting an Access table to Word

You can export an Access table to Microsoft Word by using the Publish It with MS Word feature. To export a table, open the Access database with the table you want to export, click the table, click **Tools** on the menu bar, point to **Office Links**, then click **Publish It with MS Word**. An Access wizard automatically opens Word, exports the table data, and creates a new table with the database information.

Practice

▶ Independent Challenges

1. As the administrator for Monroe High School, you want to keep track of student records and generate reports for the principal and school district. You need to create a database containing the current students enrolled in the high school. Once the database table is complete, export the table information to Excel and Word to create reports.

To complete this independent challenge:

1. Decide what fields should be included in the database. Include fields for student's name, address, phone number, gender (male or female), birth date, race, grade level, and cumulative grade point average (GPA).
2. Save the new database file as Student Records then create the student table called Student Info.
3. Create a form to facilitate the entry of your student records, then print one record to show a sample of the form.
4. Add 20 records to your table drawing on names in your local area, then sort the students by last name and then by first name.
5. Export the Student Info table to an Excel worksheet, then resize columns to fit the table.
6. Print out your results, then save the worksheet as Student Profiles to your Student Disk.
7. Export the Student Info table to a Word table, resize columns to fit the table, sort the table by grade level and then by last name, then format the table to make the document more attractive.
8. Save the document as Student Roster to your Student Disk.
9. Submit all printed materials from this challenge.

2. Pleasantown Players, the local theater group that you manage, wants to send a letter to patrons in the database encouraging them to financially support the upcoming session. To maximize your results, you decide to send out the initial mailing to those patrons who have donated more than $500. To complete the task, you need to modify the current Patrons table and create a query to find the appropriate patrons. Once the database query is complete, create a form letter in which you will merge the data stored in the query.

To complete this independent challenge:

1. Create a new database using the Donations Database Wizard.
2. Save the new database file as Pleasantown Players to your Student Disk.
3. Use default settings and include sample data as you step through the Donations Database Wizard.
4. Create a query to find patrons who have donated over $500 called Patrons over $500.
5. Create a main document (form letters) in Word using all the fields you feel are necessary.
6. In the letter, you want to tell patrons how important it is to support local, non-professional theater. Add a paragraph that briefly summarizes the number and location of non-professional theater companies like Pleasantown Players around the country. To find this information, log on to the Internet and use your browser to go to http://www.course.com. From there, click Student On Line Companions, and then click the link to go to the Microsoft Office 97 Professional Edition—Illustrated: A First Course page, then click the Integration link for Unit B. Click the link there to find the number of shows the average non-professional theater company produces per year, and compare Pleasantown Players to that. Use any of the information you find at this Web site to add credibility and interest to your funding request.
7. Save the main document as 5 Star Support Form to your Student Disk.
8. Merge the document 5 Star Support Form and the Patrons over $500 query into a new document named 5 Star Patron Support.
9. Print the first five merged documents in 5 Star Patron Support.

Integrating
Word, Excel, Access, and PowerPoint

Objectives

► **Insert a Word outline into a PowerPoint presentation**
► **Embed a Word table into a PowerPoint slide**
► **Embed an Excel chart into a PowerPoint slide**
► **Link an Excel worksheet to a PowerPoint slide**
► **Update a linked Excel worksheet in PowerPoint**
► **Export a PowerPoint presentation to Word**

PowerPoint, the fourth component of Microsoft Office, can be easily integrated with the other Office programs. For example, to help you develop a PowerPoint presentation, you can insert a document from Word or embed objects like a Word table or an Excel worksheet directly into the slides of your presentation. An embedded object is one that is created in one program, known as a **source program**, and then stored as an independent file in another program, such as your PowerPoint presentation. ◤━━ In this unit, Lynn Shaw, the executive assistant to the president, creates a small company status presentation that will be used at this year's annual business meeting. To complete the presentation, Lynn gathers some data herself and collects more from various Nomad Ltd divisions. Because everyone at Nomad Ltd uses Microsoft Office, Lynn knows all the files are compatible.

Integration

Inserting a Word Outline into a PowerPoint Presentation

While it is very easy to create an outline in PowerPoint, it is unnecessary if the outline already exists in a Word document. You can easily insert a Word document into PowerPoint to create a presentation outline. When you insert the Word outline, the heading styles in the outline are converted to text levels in PowerPoint. For example, every Word paragraph with the style Heading 1 is converted to a new slide, and every Word paragraph with the style Heading 2 is converted to a subpoint under a slide title. If the outline you are inserting has no styles, the text is converted into an outline based on the structure of the document; each hard return indicates a new slide and each hard return followed by a tab indicates a subpoint. In this lesson, Lynn inserts a Word outline created by Angela Pacheco, Nomad's sales and marketing director. The outline explains Nomad's current company status.

Steps

1. Start PowerPoint and insert your Student Disk into the disk drive
   The PowerPoint startup dialog box opens.

2. Click the **Open an Existing Presentation option button**, then click **OK**
   The Open dialog box opens.

3. Open the file **INT C-1** from your Student Disk, then save it as **Company Summary** to your Student Disk

4. Make sure the Zoom text box shows 36%, click the **Restore button** in the Presentation window, click **Window** on the menu bar, then click **Fit to Page**
   The first slide of the presentation appears as shown in Figure C-1. Switch to Outline view.

5. Click the **Outline View button** 📄 to the left of the horizontal scroll bar
   You can insert a Word document in Slide view or in Outline view. The presentation currently contains two slides. Insert the information from the Word document after the Corporate Mission Statement in Slide 2.

6. Click the **Slide 2 slide icon**
   When you insert the Word document, it will begin with a new slide after the current slide.

7. Click **Insert** on the menu bar, then click **Slides from Outline**
   The Insert Outline dialog box opens.

8. Select the file **INT C-2** from your Student Disk, click **Insert**, then scroll down to see the new slides
   The Word document is inserted as six new slides. See Figure C-2. Once an outline is inserted into a presentation, you can edit it as if it had been created in PowerPoint. Switch to Slide view to see the slides you just inserted.

Time To

✔ Save

9. Double-click the **Slide 3 slide icon** to switch to Slide view, then click the **Next Slide button** 🔽 below the vertical scroll bar five times to view the new slides

FIGURE C-1: Lynn's slide presentation

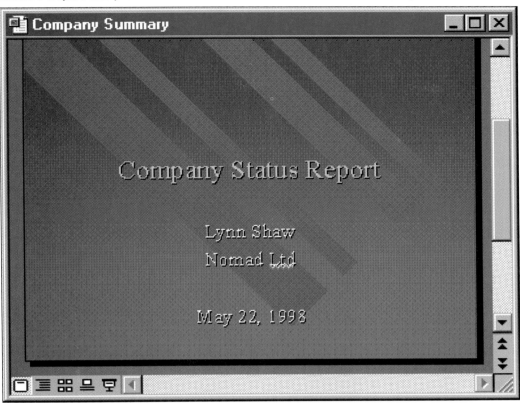

FIGURE C-2: New slides inserted in Outline view

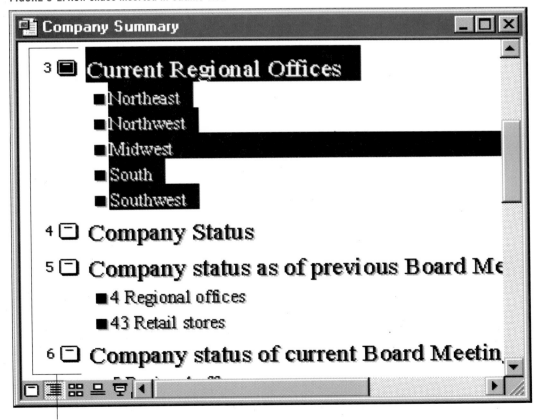

Slides 3 through 6
inserted after Slide 2

Integration

Integration

Embedding a Word Table into a PowerPoint Slide

You can create and embed a new Word table in your presentation without leaving PowerPoint. This is similar to using Microsoft Graph to insert a graph into a PowerPoint slide. Make sure to view the CourseHelp for this lesson before completing the steps. ✎ Lynn wants to create a table illustrating the growth of Nomad Ltd over the last two years.

QuickTip

You can embed an existing Word table by copying it from Word and then pasting it into PowerPoint.

1. Drag the **vertical scroll box** to Slide 4, press and hold **[Shift]** and click the main text placeholder, then press **[Delete]**

2. Click the **Insert Microsoft Word Table button** 🔲 on the Standard toolbar, then drag to create a **3 × 3 table**
   A blank Microsoft Word table is inserted in the slide, and the PowerPoint menu bar and toolbars are replaced with Word's menu and toolbars.

3. Drag the table down so it is centered between the title text and the bottom of the slide

4. Enter the information in Figure C-3 into your blank table
   Use [Tab] to move from cell to cell in your table. Now format the table using Word's formatting capabilities. First add border lines to the first row in the table.

5. Drag to select the three cells in the top row of the table, click **Format** on the menu bar, then click **Borders and Shading**
   The Borders and Shading dialog box opens with the Borders tab on top.

6. In the Style section, click the **Width list arrow**, click **3 pt**, then click at the **top** and the **bottom** of the Preview diagram as shown in Figure C-4

7. Click **OK**
   A 3 point line appears above and below the first row, although it is difficult to see it while the table is still selected. Now format the column titles.

8. On the Formatting toolbar, click the **Font list arrow**, click **Arial**, click the **Font Size list arrow**, click **36**, then click the **Center button** 🔲 on the Formatting toolbar
   The top row is set apart from the rest of the table, making it easier to read. Now format the bottom two rows.

9. Drag to select the bottom two rows of the table, click the **Outside Border list arrow** on the Formatting toolbar, click the **Bottom Border button** 🔲, click the **Font Size list arrow**, click **28**, then click 🔲
   Because the slide's shaded background is dark blue, make the text in the table white.

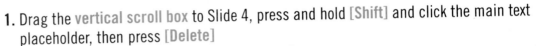

Time To
✔ Save

10. Drag to select all of the text in the table, click **Format** on the menu bar, click **Font**, click the **Color list arrow**, click **White**, click **OK**, then click a blank area of the Presentation window to deselect the table object
    Compare your screen to Figure C-5.

FIGURE C-3: Microsoft Word table

1996·Status¤	1997·Status¤	1998·Status¤
2·Regional·Offices¤	4·Regional·Offices¤	5·Regional·Offices¤
22·Retail·Stores¤	43·Retail·Stores¤	74·Retail·Stores¤

FIGURE C-4: Borders and Shading dialog box

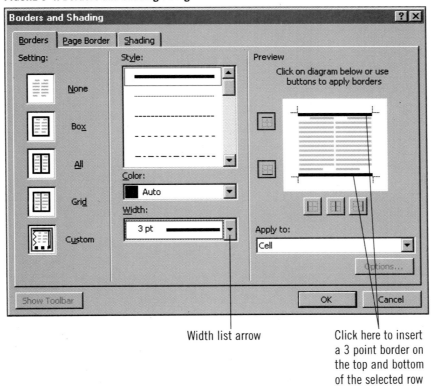

Width list arrow

Click here to insert
a 3 point border on
the top and bottom
of the selected row

FIGURE C-5: Microsoft Word table on slide

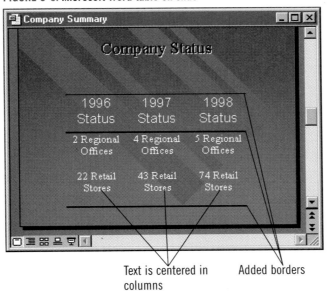

Text is centered in
columns

Added borders

Embedding an Excel Chart into a PowerPoint Slide

A powerful feature of all Microsoft Office programs is their ability to share existing information. For example, you can easily insert information from an existing Word or Excel file into a PowerPoint presentation. The information becomes an **embedded** object in PowerPoint, making it independent from its original source file. If you want to modify an embedded object, you double-click it and the original program in which the file was created opens. ✎ Lynn includes in her presentation an Excel chart that she received from Evan Brillstein in the Accounting division. After she adds the chart to her presentation, Lynn wants to format it, so she decides to embed the chart.

1. Click the **Previous Slide button** ⬆ to move to Slide 3, click **Slide Layout** on the Common Tasks toolbar, click the **Text & Object layout** (fourth row, first column), then click **Apply**

2. Double-click the object placeholder
   The Insert Object dialog box opens. You will create an embedded object from an existing file.

CourseHelp

The camera icon indicates there is a CourseHelp available with this lesson. Click the Start button, point to Programs, point to CourseHelp, then click PowerPoint 97 Illustrated. Choose the CourseHelp that corresponds to this lessson.

3. Click the **Create from file option button**, click **Browse**, click the **Look in list arrow**, click the drive containing your Student Disk, click **INT C-3**, click **OK**, then click **OK** in the Insert Object dialog box
   The Excel chart appears on the slide. Now increase the size of the chart so it is easier to see on the slide.

4. Drag the upper-left sizing handle up and to the left until the dotted line is approximately ¼" below the title text as shown in Figure C-6

5. Click the **Fill Color list arrow** on the Drawing toolbar, then click the **white square**
   Next, make the title of the chart larger. To do this, open the chart in Excel.

Trouble?

If the Excel chart toolbar appears when you try to resize the chart object, click in the Presentation window outside the chart object, then click the chart object once to select it and try Step 4 again.

6. Double-click the worksheet object
   The PowerPoint menu bar and toolbars are replaced with the Excel menu bar and toolbars, and the Excel Chart toolbar appears. If the Chart toolbar does not appear, click View on the menu bar, point to Toolbars, then click Chart.

7. Click the **Chart Objects list arrow** on the Chart toolbar, click **Chart title**, click the **Font Size list arrow** on the Formatting toolbar, and click **36**
   The change in the Excel chart is reflected in the embedded object in PowerPoint. Because this is an embedded object, editing the object does not alter the original Excel file.

QuickTip

Press [Alt] while you are resizing and repositioning the object to make your changes more precisely.

8. Click in the Presentation window outside the chart object to deselect it and return to PowerPoint

9. Click the text box with the bulleted list to select it, then drag it over to the left so that there is only approximately ¼" space between the bullets and the left side of the slide

Time To
✔ Save

10. Click the chart object once to select it, drag the left and bottom resize handles to resize the chart as large as possible as shown in Figure C-8, then click in the Presentation window outside the chart object to deselect it

FIGURE C-6: Resizing the chart object

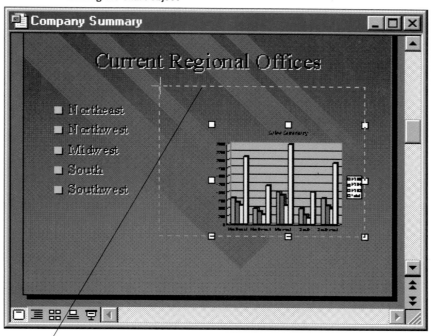

Top border of
resizing box

FIGURE C-7: Excel object embedded in slide

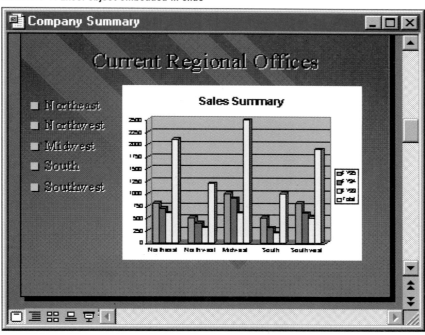

CLUES TO USE

Embedding objects using Paste Special

You can also embed an object or selected information from another Microsoft Office program into PowerPoint by copying and pasting the information. For example, assume you want to embed a worksheet from a Microsoft Excel file. Open the Microsoft Excel file that contains the worksheet, select the worksheet, and copy it to the Clipboard. Open your PowerPoint presentation, click Edit on the menu bar, click Paste Special, then click OK in the Paste Special dialog box.

Integration

Linking an Excel Worksheet to a PowerPoint Slide

Objects can also be connected to your presentation by establishing a link between the file that created the object and the PowerPoint presentation that displays the object. Unlike an embedded object which is stored directly in a slide, a linked object is stored in its original file (called the **source file**). When you **link** an object to a PowerPoint slide, a representation, or picture, of the object appears on the slide instead of the actual object, and this representation of the object is connected, or linked, to the original file. Changes made to a linked object's source file are reflected in the linked object. Some of the objects that you can link to PowerPoint include movies, PowerPoint slides from other presentations, and Microsoft Excel worksheets. See Table C-1 for information to help you decide whether to link or embed an object. ✒️═══ Lynn needs to insert an Excel worksheet created by Michael Belmont in the New Directions Travel division into her presentation. Michael saved the worksheet to Nomad's company network of computers. Lynn decides to link the worksheet because she knows Michael will have to update the worksheet before the presentation.

Steps 1234

1. Go to Slide 7, click Slide Layout on the Common Tasks toolbar, click the Text over Object layout (fifth row, fourth column), then click Apply

2. Double-click the object placeholder
   The Insert Object dialog box opens. You want to create an embedded object from an existing file.

3. Click the Create from file option button, click Browse, click the Look in list arrow, click the drive containing your Student Disk, click New Directions Profit, click OK, then click the Link check box in the Insert Object dialog box
   Compare your Insert Object dialog box to Figure C-8.

4. Click OK
   The Excel worksheet is linked to the PowerPoint slide. Now format the object to make it easier to read.

Trouble?

If Excel opens while you are trying to resize or move the worksheet, click the Close button in the Excel program window.

5. Drag the corner resize handles and reposition the worksheet object until it is approximately the same size and in the same position as in Figure C-9
   Next, change the background color so you can see the type.

6. Click the Fill Color list arrow on the Drawing toolbar, click Automatic, then click in a blank area of the Presentation window to deselect the object
   Compare your screen to Figure C-9.

7. Save your work

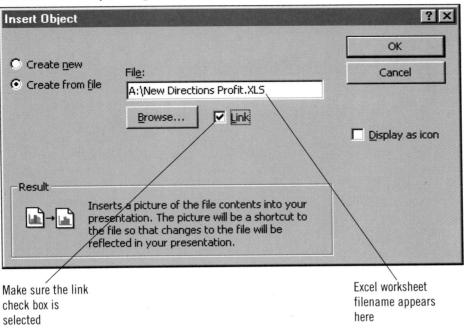

FIGURE C-8: Insert Object dialog box

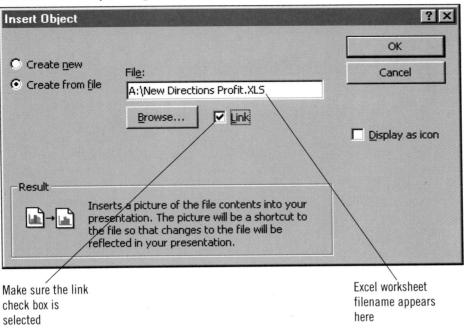

Make sure the link check box is selected

Excel worksheet filename appears here

Integration

FIGURE C-9: Linked Excel worksheet on slide

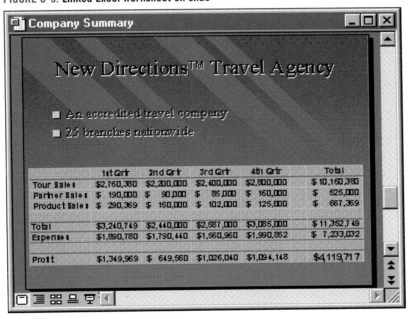

TABLE C-1: Embedding vs. Linking

situation	action
When you are the only user of an object and you want the object to be a part of your presentation	Embed
When you want to access the object in its source application, even if the original file is not available	Embed
When you want to update the object manually while working in PowerPoint	Embed
When you always want the latest information in your object	Link
When the object's source file is shared on a network or where other users have access to the file and can change it	Link
When you want to keep your presentation file size small	Link

Updating a Linked Excel Worksheet in PowerPoint

To edit or change the information in a linked object, you must open the object's source file. For example, you must start Microsoft Excel, then open the original worksheet to edit the worksheet you linked to the presentation. You can open the object's source file and the program it was created in by double-clicking the linked object. When you modify a linked object's source file, it is automatically updated in the linked presentation each time you open it. ✐ Michael needs to update the linked worksheet because the wrong number was reported for Product Sales for the third quarter.

Steps

QuickTip

To edit or open a linked object in your presentation, the object's source program and source file must be available on your computer or network.

1. **Double-click the worksheet object**
   Microsoft Excel opens in a small window in the middle of the screen, displaying the linked worksheet, and the Excel icon appears on the Taskbar.

2. **Double-click cell D4, edit the entry to 110000, click the Enter button ✓, click the Close button in the Excel program window, then click Yes to save the changes**
   Microsoft Excel closes and the linked Excel worksheet shows the change you made in Excel. Compare your screen to Figure C-10. Now check the spelling in the presentation and save your changes.

3. **Click the Spelling button 🗹 on the Standard toolbar and correct any spelling errors in the presentation**

4. **Click the Save button 🖫 on the Standard toolbar to save the changes you made**
   Switch to Slide Sorter view.

5. **Click the Slide Sorter View button 🖽 to the left of the horizontal scroll bar, click the Maximize button in the Presentation window, click the Zoom list arrow, then click 50%**
   Compare your screen to Figure C-11. Now view the final slide show and evaluate your presentation.

6. **Click Slide 1, then click the Slide Show button 🖵 to view the final presentation**
   Now print the slides of your presentation.

7. **Click File on the menu bar, click Print, click the Black & White check box to select it, then click Print to print the slides**

FIGURE C-10: Modifications reflected in linked chart

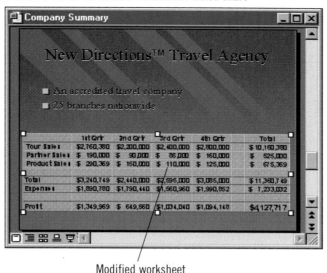

Modified worksheet
data

FIGURE C-11: The final presentation in Slide Sorter view

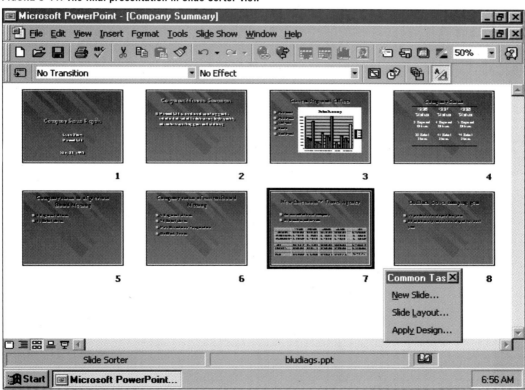

CLUES TO USE

Updating links

If the PowerPoint file is closed when you change the source file, the linked object will still reflect the changes you make to the source file. When you open the file containing the linked object, a dialog box appears reminding you that the file contains links and asking if you want to update the links now. Click OK to update the links or Cancel to leave the linked object unchanged. If you choose Cancel, you can still update the link later. Click Edit on the menu bar, then click Links to open the Links dialog box. Click the file name of the link you want to update, then click Update Now.

Integration

Exporting a PowerPoint Presentation to Word

You can export a PowerPoint presentation to Word. When you choose the Send To Microsoft Word command on the File menu, Word starts and the current PowerPoint presentation's outline exports to Word as a Word document. You can choose one of five layouts for the Word document. Once the PowerPoint outline is in Word, you can save and edit the document. ✏ Lynn wants to create handouts with blank lines so the audience can take notes during the presentation.

1. Click the Black and White View button 🖼 on the Standard toolbar
The black type does not show up very well on the dark gray background stripes.

2. Click Format on the menu bar, click Background, click the Omit background graphics from master check box to select it, then click Apply to All
Now send the file to Word.

3. Click File on the menu bar, point to Send To, then click Microsoft Word
The Write-Up dialog box appears. See Figure C-12.

4. Click the Blank lines next to slides option button
Link the presentation in case it changes before you create your handouts.

5. Click the Paste link option button

6. Click OK
Microsoft Word opens and the slides appear in a table in a new document. This process may take a little while.

7. Click the Maximize button on the Word program window, then scroll up to page 1
See Figure C-13. The slide numbers are in the first column, the slides are in the second column, and blank lines appear next to the slides in the third column. There are three slides per page. Make the slide numbers bold.

8. Select the first column, then click the Bold button 🅱 on the Formatting toolbar
Now save and print the handouts.

9. Save the file as Handouts for Company Summary to your Student Disk, then click the Print button 🖨 on the Standard toolbar
The handouts print.

10. Click the Close button on the Word program window, then click the Close button on the PowerPoint program window without saving any changes
The programs close. Do not save changes when prompted by the alert box.

FIGURE C-12: Write-Up dialog box

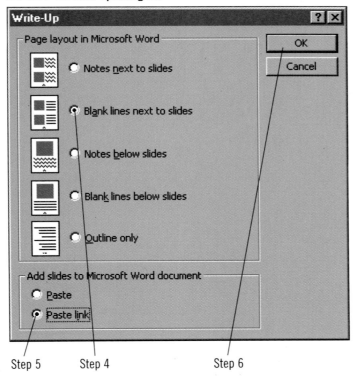

Step 5   Step 4   Step 6

FIGURE C-13: Exported PowerPoint presentation in Word

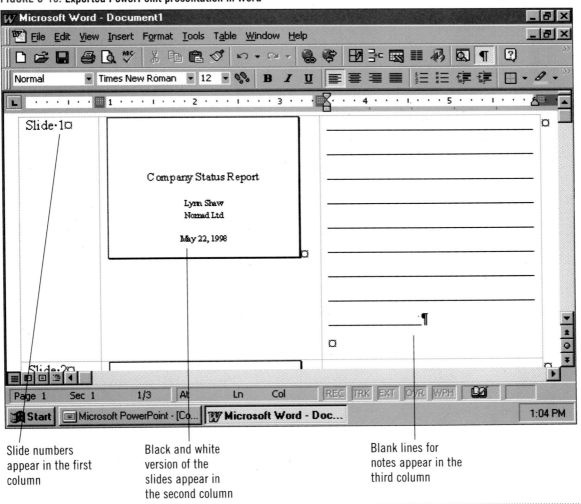

Slide numbers   Black and white   Blank lines for
appear in the first version of the   notes appear in the
column   slides appear in   third column
                     the second column

► Independent Challenges

1. You are the person in your company who recommends which software packages should be purchased. You have decided to recommend Microsoft Office. Create a PowerPoint presentation illustrating the advantages of each application in the Microsoft Office suite. Your presentation should contain slides that show how first-time computer users feel about computers and why Microsoft Office is a good choice for them. This information is provided in the file INT C-4 on your Student Disk. Think about what you would like the presentation to say and what graphics you will use. Be prepared to make an on-screen presentation to the class.

To complete this independent challenge:

1. Plan your presentation, determining its purpose and the look you want that will help communicate your message. Sketch on paper how you want the slides to look.
2. Create a PowerPoint presentation and save it as Office Review to your Student Disk.
3. Insert the Word document INT C-4 from your Student Disk into your presentation outline. This file contains information about how first-time computer users feel about computers. Use this outline to help you create your presentation. Your presentation should contain at least 10 slides.
4. Create the title slide for your presentation, then save your work.
5. Add slide show special effects, such as builds and transitions, into the presentation.
6. Check the spelling in your presentation.
7. Run the slide show and evaluate your presentation. Is your message clear? Are the slides visually appealing? Make any changes necessary and save the presentation.
8. Print the slides and outline of your presentation.
9. Submit your presentation plan and printed presentation. Be prepared to present your slide show to the class.

2. To augment the Census Bureau's data on marriage and birth-rate statistics, you have been asked to prepare a PowerPoint presentation that will run continuously at the local census office. Charts on the data need to be linked to PowerPoint slides because data is occasionally updated. Use the data found in the two worksheets in the Excel file INT C-5 on your Student Disk. Create a presentation that explains this data.

To complete this independent challenge:

1. Open the file INT C-5 from your Student Disk, then save it as Statistics to your Student Disk.
2. Create at least four charts using the data in the Marriages worksheet.
3. Create one chart using the data in the Birthrates worksheet.
4. Decide which aspects of the data you want to highlight, and write two to three paragraphs describing how your presentation will illustrate the importance of the data.
5. Create a new Word document containing an outline for your presentation, then save it as Stat Outline to your Student Disk. Print this outline.
6. Open a new PowerPoint presentation. Save it as Bureau on your Student Disk.
7. Create a title slide for the presentation.
8. Insert the Word outline into the presentation.
9. Add slide show special effects, such as builds and transitions, to the slides.
10. Link the four charts in the Marriages worksheet to slides in the presentation.
11. Embed the chart in the Birthrates worksheet in a slide in the presentation.

12. Create handouts in Word so the audience can take notes. Link the presentation in case you make changes. Save this file as Bureau Handouts to your Student Disk.

13. Check the spelling in your presentation, then run the final slide show and evaluate your presentation. Make any changes necessary.

14. Save and print the slides of your presentation.

15. After you have saved the final presentation, go back to Bureau Handouts in Word, update the link, then save and print the document. (*Hint*: To update the link, use the Links command on the Edit menu.)

16. Submit your presentation plan and printed presentation. Be prepared to present your slide show to the class.

17. Close all open applications.

3. You have been hired as an associate in the Marketing Department at Nomad Ltd. Nomad recently completed a big marketing campaign promoting its bicycle tours, but the company neglected its nonbicycle tours. Sales of the bungee jumping tours especially have fallen off. It is your job to develop a marketing strategy to restore the sales levels of non-bicycle tours. The Nomad Board of Directors, concerned about the falling sales, has suggested adding rock climbing and jeep tours to the Nomad tour line to broaden Nomad's customer base.

You decide to send a questionnaire to customers who have taken the bungee jumping tour to ask how this tour can be improved. You also decide to create a PowerPoint presentation that suggests advertising strategies for promoting the new tours. You will need several charts to show the current nonbicycle tour trends and the potential sales for the new tours.

To complete this independent challenge:

1. Start Word and open the file INT C-6 from your Student Disk. Save it as Cover Letter to your Student Disk. This is the cover letter to the questionnaire.

2. Use the Insert Picture command to add the Nomad Ltd logo to the header of the memo. The logo is in the file NOMAD on your Student Disk.

3. Start Access and open the file Customer Data from your Student Disk.

4. Create a query that lists customers who have taken the bungee tour. Save the query as "Bungee Customers".

5. Use Word's Mail Merge feature to merge the cover letter and the Access query you have created. Print the resulting letters.

6. Start Excel and open the file INT C-7 from your Student Disk. Save it as Tour Type to your Student Disk. This worksheet contains data for road bike, mountain bike, and bungee tour sales.

7. Create two charts: one that compares the sales numbers of the tours and the other that shows the tours as a percentage of all tours. Use drawing tools and color, if appropriate, to point out weak sales. Name this worksheet Current.

8. Copy the data from the Current worksheet to a new worksheet. In the new worksheet, add a formula that calculates an increase in the bungee tour sales by 20%, then show this increase in your charts. Use drawing tools and color, if appropriate, to indicate which figures are speculative. Name this worksheet Bungee Increase.

9. Copy the increased bungee tour sales data to another new worksheet, then add two more rows for the rock climbing and jeep tours. Assume their sales equal the sales of the increased bungee tour sales. Create two more charts to show the new tours. Use drawing tools and color, if appropriate, to indicate which figures are speculative and to point out the new tours. Name this worksheet New Tours.

10. Add titles to all three charts to identify them. Use drop shadows and other formatting effects to make them more attractive.

11. Print the data and the charts on all three worksheets.

12. Start PowerPoint and create a new presentation. Save it as Tour Evaluation to your Student Disk. This presentation will illustrate your marketing ideas to increase sales.

13. Create a title slide.

14. Insert the Word outline INT C-8 from your Student Disk after the title slide.
15. Add to the outline your own ideas on how to strengthen bungee tours sales and generate new sales for the new tours. You can suggest additional tours, too.
16. Include the Excel charts on your slides by using the method you feel is best: pasting, linking, or embedding, or a combination of the three.
17. Use templates, clip art, builds, and any other PowerPoint features you want to create an effective and professional-looking presentation.
18. Print the presentation as Handouts (6 slides per page).
19. Submit all your work.

4. One of your jobs at Bolten Industries is to create a presentation on the company's inventory for the yearly report. Bolten Industries produces five specialized aircraft parts for most of the U.S. jet aircraft manufacturers. The annual report needs to show how many parts, or units, were manufactured during the last year and how many were distributed to aircraft manufacturers. The presentation needs to list each aircraft manufacturer, the number of parts they received, and the cost per unit.

You decide to create a 10- to 15-slide presentation that displays all the inventory information for your report. You will need to create all the information for this challenge on your own. To help you create this presentation, assume the following:

- The five aircraft parts Bolten manufactures are the following: (1) 2-stage hydraulic nose gear assembly; (2) door lifter assemblies; (3) wing balance plates; (4) main cargo assembly lifters; (5) hydraulic lifter gears
- Bolten Industries makes parts for the following companies: Boeing, McDonnell Douglas, Lockheed, Cessna, and Learjet

To complete this independent challenge:

1. Create a database in Access using the Inventory Wizard. Enter data in all the database fields using the five aircraft parts listed above. Save the database as Parts Data to your Student Disk.
2. Create an outline in Word that you can insert into PowerPoint to use as your presentation outline. Identify 10 slides and subpoints you want on each slide in the outline and then save the Word outline as Parts Outline.
3. Insert the Word outline into a new PowerPoint presentation. Save the presentation as Bolten Inventory.
4. Create queries from the Parts Data database that list the number of parts manufactured and distributed during the last year, then create at least two Excel worksheets with the information. Embed the worksheets into the Bolten Inventory presentation.
5. Create an Excel worksheet, using your own data and showing revenue data produced by the sale of the company's aircraft parts. Save the workbook as Aircraft Parts Revenue. Link the worksheet to PowerPoint.
6. Use templates, clip art, builds, and any other PowerPoint features you want to create an effective and professional-looking presentation. To find photographs, log on to the Internet and use your browser to go to http://www.course.com. From there, click the link Student OnLine Companions, then click Microsoft Office 97 Professional Edition—Illustrated: A First Course page, then click the Integration link for Unit C. You can download photographs from the links found there.
   Make sure to abide by any terms and conditions for using copyrighted material at the sites. Note that when you include photographs in a presentation, you increase the size of the presentation file significantly.
7. Save and print the presentation.
8. Print out the files you created in Word and Excel.
9. Submit all the files and printouts you created.

Exploring

Integration: Word, Excel, and Internet Explorer

Objectives

► **Modify a Word document**
► **Enhance Excel data**
► **Modify a Web document**

The skills you have developed in Word and Excel make your work more efficient and your documents and worksheets more professional. You can use elements from Word and Excel to create an effective Web document. Keith Watchman, Manager of Nomad Ltd's Bookkeeping Department, is preparing information for Nomad's efforts to acquire one of three companies. Because his co-workers use Microsoft Office 97 Professional, Keith will be able to combine their files with his own files easily.

Integration

Modifying a Word Document

Nomad's Board of Directors is planning to increase its product line by acquiring an existing company. Three prospective companies have been identified, and preliminary information has been obtained about each. ▰▰▰ Keith Watchman has gathered the financial information on the prospective companies and is preparing information to present to the company Board members, accountants, and legal staff. A member of Keith's department has started a memo that Keith will use as a cover letter, incorporating spreadsheet data, for the project.

QuickTip
You can use the Insert menu or a button on the Drawing toolbar to insert WordArt.

1. **Open the Word document INT D-1, then save it as Bookkeeping Memo**
   Add WordArt to the document to make it more attractive.

2. **Delete the WordArt placeholder in the document, then create your own WordArt that reads "Bookkeeping Department," similar to the sample shown in Figure D-1**

3. **Enter information in the TO: and RE: sections of the memo using Figure D-1 as a guide**
   You received background information on each of the three companies, portions of which you want to include in your memo.

4. **Open the document INT D-2, then save it as Preliminary Research**
   Start the memo with an introductory paragraph, followed by the board's analysis of the three companies.

5. **In the Bookkeeping Memo, replace the "Enter text here" placeholder with a short introductory paragraph of your own, then copy the three bulleted items from the Preliminary Research document into the memo**
   To back up the proposal, add a section to the memo summarizing the financial data you've gathered.

6. **Open the Excel workbook INT D-3, then save it as Acquisition Data**

7. **In the Bookkeeping Memo, write a paragraph introducing the acquisition data, copy the annual totals for each company into the memo, then format the table appropriately**
   Compare your memo to the sketch in Figure D-2. Now, print and save the file.

8. **Save, preview, and print the Bookkeeping Memo, then close Word**

FIGURE D-1: Bookkeeping Memo with WordArt

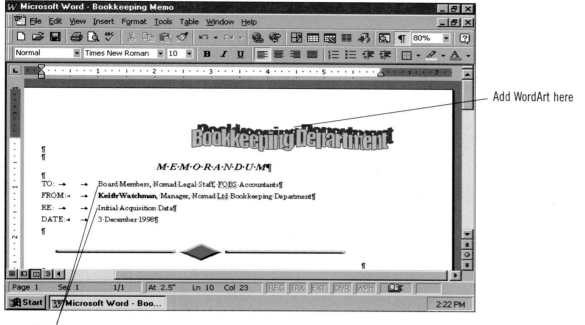

Add WordArt here

Add information
here

FIGURE D-2: Sample sketch of page layout

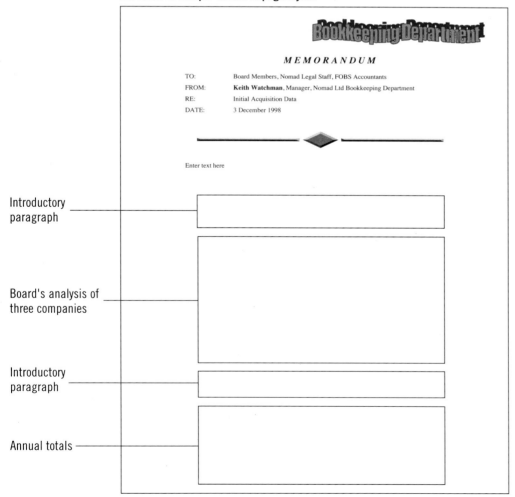

Introductory
paragraph

Board's analysis of
three companies

Introductory
paragraph

Annual totals

Enhancing Excel Data

Keith wants to increase the effectiveness of the financial data for each of the three companies under consideration. To do this, he'll format the data more attractively and convert the information to a chart. ◢◣ Keith decides to summarize the data in the Acquisition Data workbook on a single sheet. To call attention to the data, he'll use the Drawing toolbar and other techniques to format and annotate the information. Also he wants to create a chart for each company that will make the data more meaningful.

Steps

1. **Activate the Acquisition Data workbook**
   Create a summary page on a new sheet that contains all the data for each of the three companies.

2. **Insert a worksheet, rename the sheet Summary, create links so all the data on all the sheets is visible, then resize columns as necessary**
   See Figure D-3. Enhance the data using AutoFormats and the Drawing toolbar.

3. **Apply an AutoFormat of your choice to the data on the Summary sheet, then add annotations (circles, arrows, and text) where appropriate**
   Now you are ready to create charts for the data. You want the charts to appear on a new first sheet in the workbook, instead of on the Summary sheet.

4. **Insert a worksheet, then rename the sheet Charts**
   You want to create charts that illustrate the sales history of each company.

5. **Create one 3-D column chart for each company's data**
   Include any chart enhancements you feel are appropriate. Compare your work to Figure D-4. Next, you want to create a report that prints only the sheets containing the charts and the summary information.

6. **Use the Report Manager to create a report titled Graphic Summary that includes the Summary and Charts sheets and is numbered continuously**

7. **Save the workbook, then print the Graphic Summary report**

QuickTip

The Report Manager is an Excel feature that will only be available if it has been installed. See your instructor if this feature is not available.

FIGURE D-3: Summary sheet in Acquisition Data workbook

Results of linking formulas

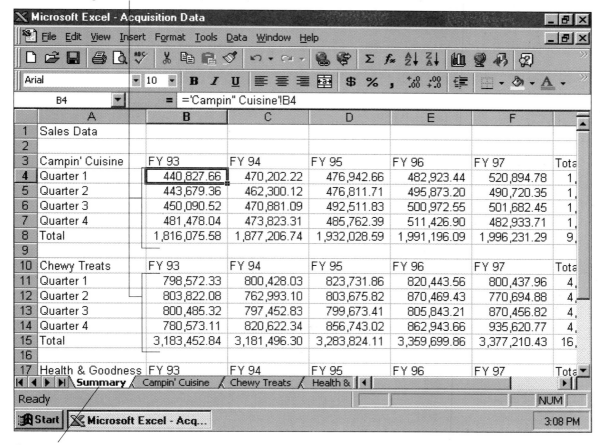

Newly added sheet

FIGURE D-4: Sample financial data charts

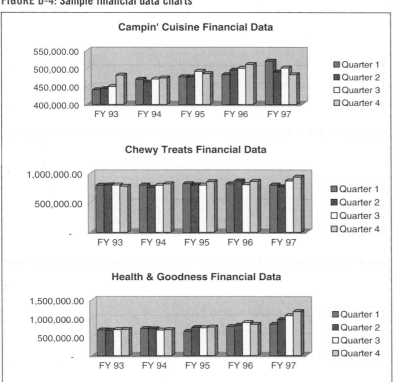

Integration

Modifying a Web Document

Because Nomad Ltd wants to keep its employees up-to-date on the impending acquisition, the Nomad Webmaster has established a page that the bookkeeping department maintains to make sure employees have current information. Nomad employees read this page to keep current on acquisition news. ✒ Keith will incorporate Excel charts from his memo into his department's existing Web page.

Steps 1 2 3 4

1. Open the Word HTML document INT D-4, then save it as **Acquisition Updates**
First, replace a placeholder with explanatory text.

2. Select the text **Type some text**, then type **Sales histories of potential acquisitions**
Compare your document to Figure D-5.
Next, you copy Excel charts from the Acquisition Data workbook into this page.

3. Activate the Charts sheet in the **Acquisition Data workbook**
Use the Copy button to copy the Campin' Cuisine chart.

4. Click the Campin' Cuisine chart, then click the **Copy button** 📋 on the Standard toolbar
Once you have copied data to the Clipboard, you can paste it into another document using the Paste button.

5. Activate the **Acquisition Updates** document, select the line containing **Copy Campin' Cuisine chart here**, then click the **Paste button** 📋 on the Standard toolbar

6. Replace the remaining chart placeholders with the charts in the Acquisition Data workbook
Once the charts are pasted in the Web page, save your work.

7. Click the **Save button** 💾 on the Standard toolbar
With your work saved, preview the modified page using your Web browser, Microsoft Internet Explorer.

8. Click the **Web Page Preview button** 🔍 on the Standard Web toolbar, then click the **Print button** 🖨 on the Internet Explorer toolbar
Compare your printout to Figure D-6.

FIGURE D-5: Web page with text added

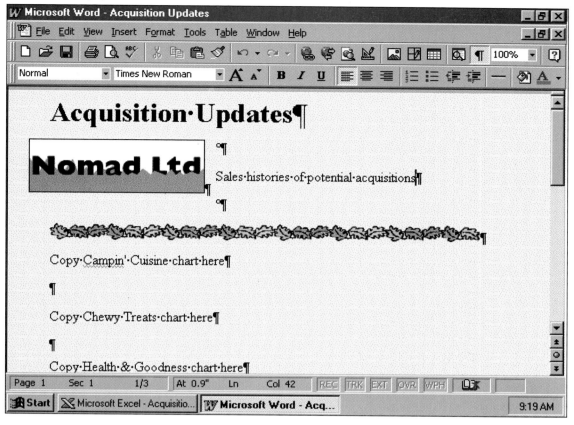

FIGURE D-6: Printed Web page

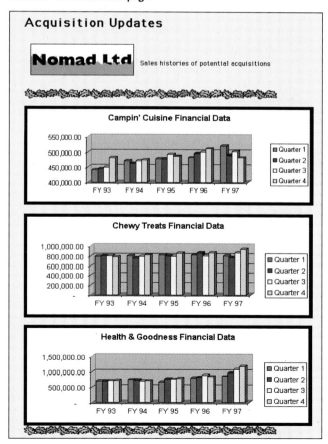

▶ Independent Challenges

1. You've decided to act on your lifelong interest in botany and start your own floral shop called My Green Thumb. During your initial discussion with a banker from Big Bucks Bank, you were asked to submit a budget of anticipated expenses and revenues, as well as a one-page proposal outlining your plans for building the business. You are seeking a $25,000 startup business loan, which your banker assured you should be approved. Because the bank has Internet access, you've decided to create a Web page and include a printout of it in your loan application.

To complete this independent challenge:

1. Open the workbook INT D-5, then save it as "My Green Thumb Budget."
2. Create your own expense data using this workbook as a guide. Add more expenses if you wish.
3. Sort the expenses alphabetically, then create formulas to calculate quarterly and annual expenses.
4. Rename Sheet 2 "Income." Create a worksheet that calculates anticipated monthly, quarterly, and annual revenue.
5. Create a letterhead document for your company, then save it as "My Green Thumb Letterhead." Create a WordArt company logo for the letterhead, and include any applicable Clipart.
6. Use the letterhead to write your proposal, and save it as "My Green Thumb Proposal."
7. Compose a cover letter to the bank titled "Big Bucks Bank Cover Letter."
8. Create a Web page using the Web Page Wizard called "My Green Thumb web page." Add the logo you created and any other information or artwork to make the page look professional.
9. Save, preview, then print the documents you created.
10. Submit your printed materials.

2. Recently, you started managing the Great Ghouls Costume Shop, which rents costumes to both groups and individuals. In anticipation of Halloween, you've decided to host a gala costume party for current customers. Since you want your customers to come as their favorite horror show characters, you search the World Wide Web (WWW) for some suggestions.

To complete this independent challenge:

1. Create a Word document that contains a list of 15 costumes your company carries. Save the document as "Great Ghouls Costumes."
2. Create a Word document that announces your Halloween party. Save it as "Great Ghouls Costume Party." Add Clipart and WordArt to make the document more attractive.
3. Open the workbook INT D-6, then save it as "Great Ghouls Stock."
4. Log on to the Internet and use your Web browser to go to http://www.course.com. From there, click Student Online Companions, click the link for this textbook, then click on the Integration link for Unit D.
5. Use any of the following sites to compile your data about characters in horror movies: Shrine to Jason, Psycho, the Hannibal Lecter Home Page, or any other site you can find with related information.
6. Use information on the Web to create a list of costumes.
7. Copy the list of costumes from the Great Ghouls Costumes document to the Great Ghouls Stock workbook.
8. Supply in-stock and rental-fee figures, then format the data attractively.
9. Create a Web page to advertise your shop. Include any appropriate artwork and information.
10. Save, preview, then print your documents.
11. Submit your printed materials.

Exploring

Integration: Word, Excel, and Access

Objectives

▶ Copy an Access table into Word

▶ Sort Access data in Excel

▶ Embed an Excel chart in Word

Integrating data from multiple programs allows you to combine information from a variety of sources with valuable analytical tools and features. Nomad Ltd's bookkeeping manager, Keith Watchman, has learned that his company is close to deciding which new company it will acquire. Keith's department has been asked for further background information. Although this information is readily available, it should undergo some analysis and manipulation before it is presented to the board of directors and Nomad's accountants.

Integration

Copying an Access Table into Word

Although the company has not made a final decision, Nomad's first acquisition choice is Health & Goodness Inc. Nomad's accounting firm, FOBS, wants an analysis of the sample product line. Keith has examined the H&G products database and is analyzing it. Using Word, he will include a cover letter to the accountants that outlines the data analysis. Using the bookkeeping department's standard memo document, Keith writes a brief synopsis of the data from the Access database and encloses a short list of sample products.

Steps 1 2 3 4

1. **Open INT E-1; in the RE: memo block, type Acquisition Analysis, then save the document as Cover Letter to FOBS**
   Once the memo document is open, open the Access database table containing the needed records.

2. **Open the H&G Products database, then open the Sample Product Line table**
   The table containing sample items in the H&G product line appears. Move some of the fields to the end of the table because you don't need them now.

3. **Move the Product ID and Serial Number fields so they appear at the far right of the table, then maximize the table and resize the fields so that all the data is visible**
   As you review the table, you realize that you don't need to see all the fields. Create a query that retrieves only the necessary information.

4. **Create a query called Product Listing that displays the fields in the following order: Product Name, Product Description, Unit, and Unit Price**
   Next, modify the query so the records display in a particular order.

5. **Sort the records in descending order by Product Description, then in ascending order by Product Name**
   Compare your queried table to that shown in Figure E-1. The resulting list of products is too long to include in the memo, so you decide to filter it by adding criteria to the query.

6. **Modify the query to include only those products that have a Product ID of FO-01 or FO-02, *but do not display this field*, then save this query as Product Listing Short List**
   The modified query retrieves 12 records. You are ready to include this data in your memo.

QuickTip
"Suppliment" and "tomatos" are misspellings and will be corrected using the Spell Check feature.

7. **Spell-check the document, copy the Product Listing Short List into the Cover Letter to FOBS document, then format the table using AutoFormat**
   Compare your document to Figure E-2. Once the table data is incorporated into the memo, write a short introductory paragraph.

8. **Replace the Enter text here: placeholder with a brief paragraph that introduces the table data, then save, preview, and print the Cover Letter to FOBS**

FIGURE E-1: Queried Access table

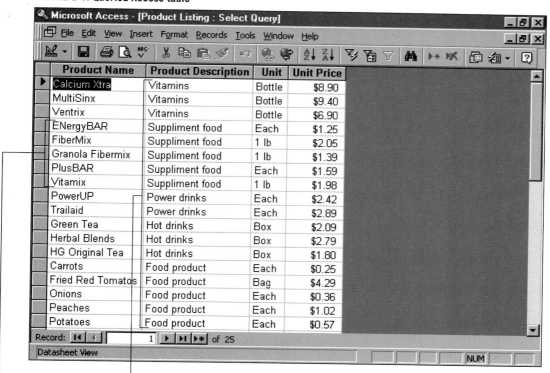

Records in ascending
order within each
product description

Records in descending
order by product
description

FIGURE E-2: Access data in Word document

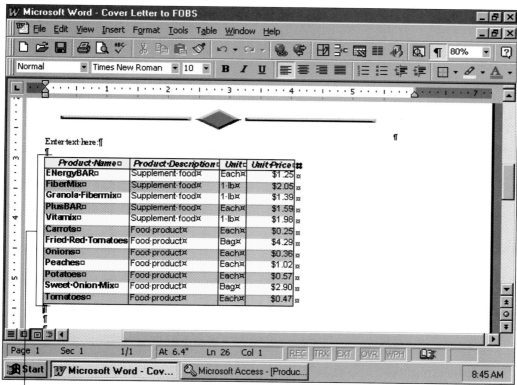

Access table copied
and formatted

Sorting Access Data in Excel

Keith will forward the information in the Access table to Nomad's accounting firm. He thinks the raw data will be stronger if it is accompanied by a product analysis. Keith will submit an analysis determining which sample products require the longest lead time. First, he'll create an Access query to retrieve the data, and then he'll use an Excel worksheet to analyze it.

Steps

1. **Create a query of the Sample Product Line table that includes the following fields: Product Name, Product Description, Unit, Reorder Level, and Lead Time**
   The query displays all the fields Keith needs for his analysis. Next, Keith adds sort criteria to the query.

2. **Sort the query in ascending order by Product Name, then save it as Product Shipping Analysis**
   You can copy datasheet information to Excel using the copy/paste method or by selecting the query in the Database window, clicking the Office Links list arrow button on the Database toolbar, then clicking Analyze It with MS Excel.

3. **Copy the query datasheet to a blank Excel workbook, then save the workbook as Product Shipping Analysis**
   Use the AutoFilter to apply criteria to the data quickly.

4. **Use AutoFilter to produce a list of products that require "2 days" lead time, as shown in Figure E-3, print the worksheet, then turn off the AutoFilter**
   AutoFilter reveals that only 6 of the 25 products need a two-day lead time. You think that a summary of the sample data information is needed.

5. **Create equations beneath the current data that determine the number of products by the lead time they require, as shown in Figure E-4**
   Chart the analysis to add emphasis to it.

6. **Create two charts of the analysis: one showing the lead times required (by product description), and the other showing the percentage of each product description in the sample**
   Compare your results to Figure E-4.

7. **Save, preview, and print the analysis and charts (in landscape orientation) in the Product Shipping Analysis worksheet**

FIGURE E-3: AutoFiltered data in Excel

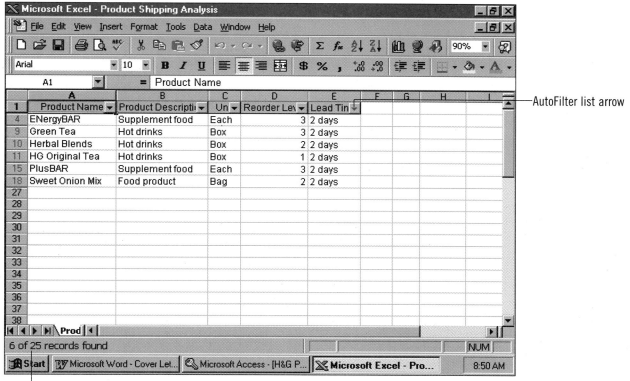

AutoFilter list arrow

Number of qualifying records

FIGURE E-4: Analysis and charts of Access table in Excel

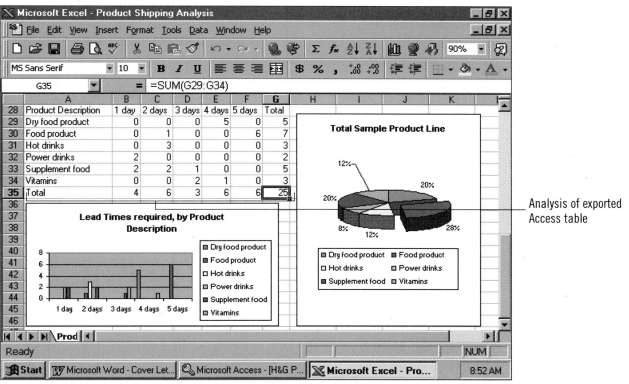

Analysis of exported Access table

Embedding an Excel Chart in Word

Documentation of mathematical data has more impact if text or numbers are accompanied by illustrations, such as charts. ◆━━━ Keith decides to include one of the charts he created. Instead of just copying and pasting the chart, however, he'll embed it. That way, if the data changes, his memo will be updated automatically.

Steps

1. **Click the chart containing the percentage of each product description**
   Once the chart is selected, copy it to the Clipboard.

2. **Click the Copy button 🖺 on the Standard toolbar**
   In order to embed the chart, return to the Word document.

3. **Activate the Cover Letter to FOBS**
   You decide to embed the chart beneath the previously copied Access table.

4. **Click two lines beneath the copied Access table query**
   Embedding the chart means that the data in the memo will be identical to the data in the Excel chart.

5. **Use the Paste Special command to embed the chart**
   You decide to add descriptive text that wraps to the right of the chart.

6. **Add a descriptive paragraph that wraps to the right of the chart**
   Compare your document to Figure E-5.

7. **Save the document, then close Word, Access, and Excel**

FIGURE E-5: Word document with embedded Excel chart

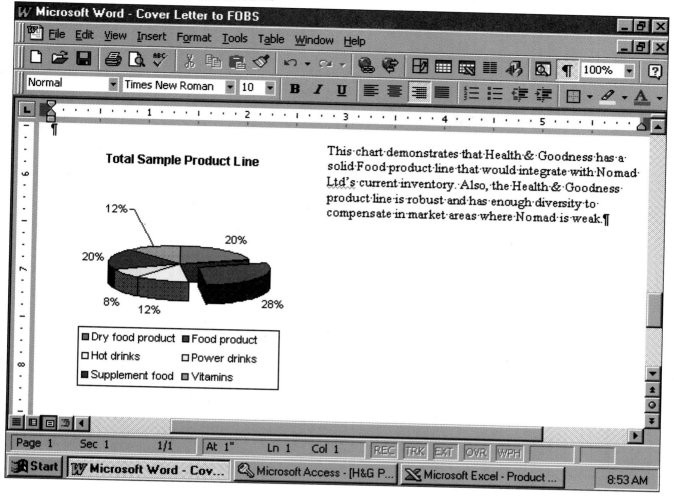

Practice

▶ Independent Challenges

1. The Big Bucks Bank approved you for a $25,000 business loan to start your new floral shop, My Green Thumb. Your company is thriving, and your inventory is expanding. Because the loan enabled you to purchase a computer containing Microsoft Office, you're interested in sending your current customers a copy of your inventory list.

To complete this independent challenge:

1. Using the My Green Thumb database file, create at least 15 items in the Product Line table.
2. Create a query called "In-Stock Items" that sorts products in ascending order and retrieves all products that have more than five items in stock.
3. Copy the results of the In-Stock Items query to a new Excel workbook.
4. Use AutoFormat to make the data more attractive.
5. Create a new table within the database file titled "Customers," then add five customer records.
6. Create a Word document titled "Letter to Green Thumb Customers" that tells customers about the list of in-stock products.
7. Merge the Customer table with the Letter to Green Thumb Customers.
8. Print the results of the mail merge, then submit your printed materials.

2. You have recently started a business called Mega-Web Sites using your personal computer (PC). This business will track Web sites pertaining to American history. Your subscribers want to be kept current on the best Web sites for a variety of historic events.

To complete this independent challenge:

1. Log on to the Internet and use your web browser to go to http://www.course.com. From there, click Student Online Companions, click the link for this textbook, then click the Integration link for Unit E.
2. Use any of the following sites to compile your data: the Library of Congress, the FDR Library, the LBJ Library and Museum, the John F. Kennedy Library, or any other site where you can find related information.
3. Create a database that contains a Web Site table with at least 10 historic Web sites in it. Save the database file as "Mega Web Sites."
4. Create a table called "Customers," and add at least five records.
5. Create a relationship between the Customers and Web Site tables.
6. Create a query that displays Web sites requested by each customer.
7. Copy the resulting datasheet into an Excel workbook titled "Web Site Info."
8. Use the AutoFilter to determine which Web sites are the most popular.
9. Create a short Word document titled "Historic Web Sites" that records your findings.
10. Combine the data compiled in Excel into the Word document.
11. Print the Web Site Info document, then submit your work.

Exploring

Integration: Office 97 Professional

Objectives

- ► **Create a presentation using a Word outline**
- ► **Add a Word table and Excel worksheet to slides**
- ► **Create relationships in Access**
- ► **Analyze Access data in Excel**
- ► **Export an Access table into Word**
- ► **Import Excel data into PowerPoint**

As the previous units have explained, Microsoft PowerPoint provides the necessary tools to create great-looking presentations. With Microsoft Office, you can use not only PowerPoint's built-in tools, but all the formatting and data analysis tools available in Microsoft Word, Excel, and Access as well to create professional, integrated presentations. While developing a presentation, it's helpful to use information you or someone else has created in other Microsoft Office programs. Because PowerPoint is a part of Microsoft Office, you can exchange files or data easily between Word, Excel, Access, and PowerPoint.

In this integration unit, Nomad Ltd is preparing to acquire Health & Goodness Inc, a dry foods corporation located in Santa Fe, New Mexico. You will help Chris Weaver of Nomad Ltd as he develops three presentations in PowerPoint using information from Access, Excel, and Word for Nomad's president, Bill Davidson.

Integration

Creating a Presentation Using a Word Outline

Once you've created an outline in Word, it's easy to build a PowerPoint presentation. This is a time-saving technique when you're using content from an existing Word document, or if you prefer creating your initial outline in Word. Then, you can focus on formatting and enhancing your presentation using PowerPoint. ✎ To get started, Chris creates a presentation using a Word outline that gives a summary of the Health & Goodness Inc (H&G) acquisition. Because this presentation is for the company division heads, it does not need to be detailed, but it should be informative and complete. To complete the presentation, Chris adds a template, plans the design of each slide, formats each slide, then sets slide builds, transitions, slide timings, and interactive settings.

1. **Open a blank PowerPoint presentation, then save it as Nomad 1**
   A blank presentation appears. Now, insert an outline from Word that you will use as the basis for the presentation.

2. **Insert the document INT F-1 into your presentation, then in Outline view make any needed changes to the text**
   Compare your screen to Figure F-1. Fill in the blank areas in the outline with your own content. You may want to change the outline flow or create some additional information about H&G that would help the target audience. Use Outline view to finalize the presentation content. Now, move to Slide view and organize the contents of each slide in the presentation.

QuickTip

For a dramatic 3-D effect, shade a slide background in one direction, then shade objects or shapes in another direction.

3. **Switch to Slide view, apply a template, then plan how you want each slide in the presentation to look**
   Use the sample sketch in Figure F-2 to help design your presentation. Take some time and look through the PowerPoint templates to the one that fits the presentation. If you don't like any of the standard templates, create one or modify an existing PowerPoint template. If you modify a PowerPoint template, make sure you rename the template and save it as a presentation template to your My Integration Files folder. During this design phase, decide how you can use clipart, drawn objects, tables, charts, sounds, movies, headers and footers, or other enhancing objects to communicate your message effectively. Analyze the content of each presentation slide to see if a chart, table, or other object could better communicate the topic you are presenting.

4. **Adjust each slide in the presentation based on your design decisions**
   You may need to change a slide's AutoLayout (for example, so the slide can accommodate a picture, chart, or movie), change master text indents, change the anchor point or spacing of text, or customize master placeholders.

FIGURE F-1: Inserted Word outline in PowerPoint

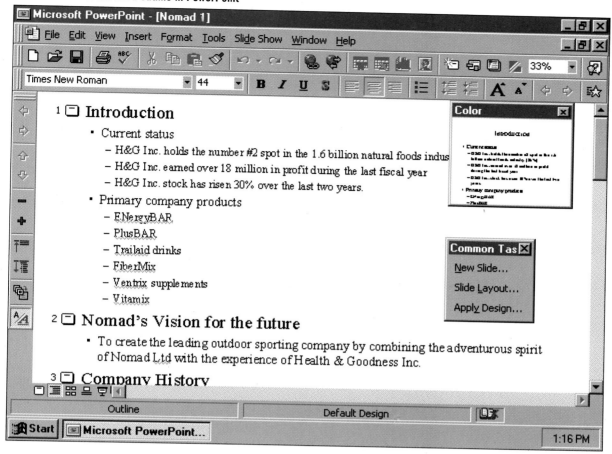

FIGURE F-2: Sample presentation sketch

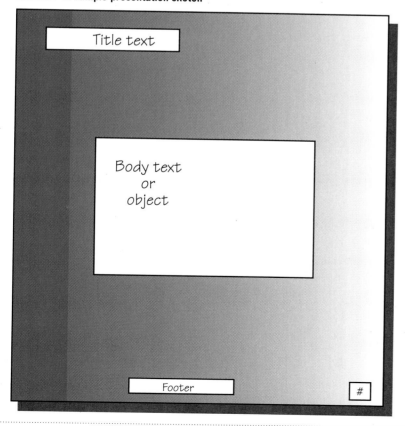

Integration

Adding a Word Table and Excel Worksheet to Slides

After you have adjusted the design of your slides, you can fine-tune each slide one at a time by adding objects and changing slide and text formatting. Sometimes, when you insert content or an outline from another source such as Microsoft Word, the text or data doesn't fit the slide design or look good in its current form. Then you need to change the slide layout or the way text or data appears on the slide to achieve a certain look. At this stage, you also will decide about adding data from other applications such as Microsoft Excel to help communicate your message. Chris finishes this presentation by customizing some of the content, embedding an Excel worksheet, then setting slide show features.

Steps

1. **Add or create objects that enhance your presentation slides**
   Use clipart, drawn objects, photographs, animation movies, digital movies, or sound to enhance your presentation. If necessary, change an object's appearance to better fit the slide color scheme or design. Be careful not to overload your presentation with too many objects; you don't want your audience distracted from the message of your presentation.

2. **Convert the text relating to H&G's primary products to an embedded Word table**
   The easiest way to convert text in PowerPoint to a Word table is to cut the text from the slide, then paste it into a Word document. Because you want to convert the text on the slide to an embedded table, first insert a Word document into your slide using the Insert Object command, then paste the text from PowerPoint to the Word document. Once the text is in Word, convert it to a table style, format the table using Word's formatting tools, then exit Word to embed the table into your presentation. Refer to the sample table shown in Figure F-3.

3. **Add a new slide called Financial Data to the presentation, then create and embed an Excel worksheet**
   Use the Excel worksheet in Figure F-4 as the basis for your data. Use formulas and the AutoSum button to calculate totals in the worksheet. Format the worksheet using Excel's formatting tools. Embed the Excel worksheet in your presentation. Once the worksheet is embedded in your presentation, you may need to scale it so it's easier to see and position it on the slide. Use PowerPoint's formatting tools to enhance the worksheet so it stands out on the slide.

4. **Finish by checking for spelling errors, then set builds, transitions, slide timings, and interactive settings for each slide in the presentation**
   Set build options in the Animation Settings dialog box for titles, main text objects, and objects. Set interactive settings options for objects you want to interact with during the slide show. For example, you might want to edit or open an embedded chart.

5. **Save, print, then close your presentation**
   Be prepared to justify your presentation design and revisions.

FIGURE F-3: Word table sketch

Product	Units Sold	Total
1. ENergyBAR	467,390 ea	$ 584,237.50
2. Trailaid drinks	187,932 ea	$ 543,123.48
3. Ventrix	59,035 btl	$ 407,341.50
4. PlusBAR	210,968 ea	$ 335,439.12
5. FiberMix	35,621 lbs	$ 73,023.05
6. Vitamix	19,004 lbs	$ 37,627.92

FIGURE F-4: Excel worksheet

H&G Sales Data	FY 93	FY 94	FY 95	FY 96	FY 97
Quarter 1	$ 693,427.83	$ 732,956.16	$ 657,933.84	$ 784,690.32	$ 848,925.77
Quarter 2	$ 688,475.09	$ 725,632.88	$ 759,437.22	$ 823,485.12	$ 973,204.72
Quarter 3	$ 700,925.98	$ 690,427.76	$ 750,832.09	$ 893,862.45	$ 1,078,940.92
Quarter 4	$ 710,473.88	$ 701,533.25	$ 770,428.10	$ 846,327.09	$ 1,186,358.32
Total	$ 2,793,302.78	$ 2,850,550.05	$ 2,938,631.25	$ 3,348,364.98	$ 4,087,429.73
5 yr Total					$ 16,018,278.79

Integration

Creating Relationships in Access

When the data you need for your presentation already exists in an Access database, you can import it into your PowerPoint presentation. You can manipulate Access data to get exactly the information you need by creating relationships between tables, then importing the information into Excel for analysis and formatting. The president of Nomad, Bill Davidson, needs to give a presentation to Nomad's Board of Directors that focuses on the benefits of acquiring H&G. The presentation should include information on H&G's top four clients. To complete this presentation, Chris uses the presentation he created for the company division heads in the last project as the basis for a new one. To get the appropriate information for this project, Chris creates a relationship between two Access tables, queries the database, analyzes the data in Excel, then imports it into a PowerPoint presentation.

Steps 1 2 3 4

1. Open the Access database H&G Inc
You need to extract client and product sales information from the second quarter of 1995 for your presentation. The database that H&G provided Nomad does not include a client table, so you add one.

2. Add a new table to the H&G Inc database, then save it as Customer List
Refer to Figures F-5 and F-6 for help in creating the new table. Remember to define the length and data type of the fields exactly as you see them in Figure F-6 to link the tables successfully. The Customer ID field in this table will link to the Customer ID field in the H&G 1997 Sales table. You need to link the tables to create a query for the presentation.

3. Create a one-to-many relationship between the H&G Inc tables
Identify the common field in each table in the database that will link the tables. To ensure data integrity, make sure you enforce referential integrity between the tables. When you have successfully linked the tables, you will see a one-to-many line between the Customer List table and the H&G 1997 Sales table and between the H&G 1997 Sales table and the H&G Products table. Now you create a query with the database tables to determine which clients are purchasing H&G's primary products.

4. Create a query using all three H&G Inc tables, use the fields in Table F-1, sort in ascending order by Company Name field, then save it as Customer Comparison
Use the Query Design View to create your query. Add the H&G Inc database tables to the Query Design View; then, if necessary, rearrange each table's field list to view its contents. Arrange the fields in a logical manner based on how you want the table to look. You might want to review the table in Query View to see how the finished table will look.

5. Export the Customer Comparison query to Microsoft Excel, then save it as Customer Comparison
Excel creates a worksheet that displays the Customer Comparison query from Access. Now that you have imported the information, you can close Access.

FIGURE F-5: Customer List Table in Design view

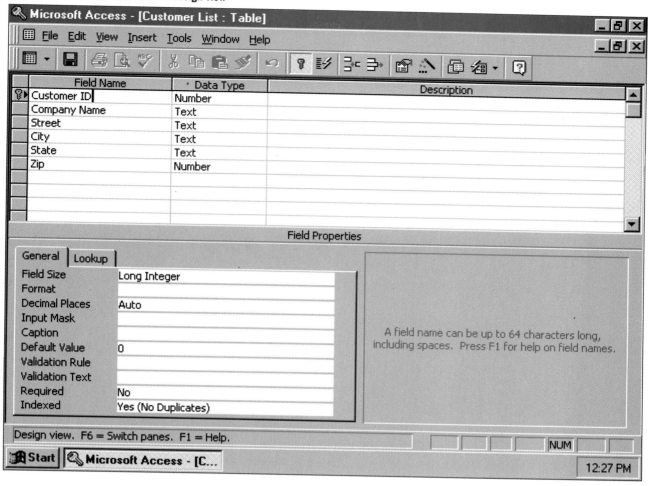

FIGURE F-6: Customer List Table

	Customer ID	Company Name	Street	City	State	Zip
	1889	CO-OP USA	8723 Front St.	L.A.	CA	93902
	2459	Western Foods Inc.	One High Ave.	Vancouver	WA	94532
	3409	Chestnut Stores	3489 Haber Rd. Suite #34	Southfork	MI	19011
	12384	Natural Products Inc.	9490 Mission Ave.	Berkeley	CA	90345
	23429	Company Square	21120 46th Ave. Flr #12	New York	NY	20090
	58938	All Natural Company	6422 Forest St.	Dun Glen	NV	82353
▶	0					0

TABLE F-1: Customer Comparison query fields

table field list name	fields in list
Customer List	Customer ID, Company Name
H&G 1997 Sales	Units Sold, Unit Price
H&G Products	Product ID, Product Name

Integration

Analyzing Access Data in Excel

Importing the database information into Excel allows Chris to analyze and format the data before exporting it to PowerPoint. For this presentation to the Board of Directors, Chris wants some specific information on H&G's top four clients. ✎ He finishes by adding a total column to the Excel worksheet, formatting the worksheet, analyzing the data, charting the analyzed data, and then embedding four charts in his PowerPoint presentation.

Steps 1 2 3 4

1. **Add a column titled Total to the worksheet, calculate the total amounts for each H&G client, then calculate the total for the entire worksheet**
   Use formulas to calculate the figures in the Total column, then format the worksheet using the AutoFormat feature. Now analyze each client's numbers using your Excel skills.

2. **Create a table that determines sales for each product**
   Use sorting or AutoFilter to create data similar to that shown in Figure F-7.

3. **Create a chart to display the data**
   Figure F-8 shows how a typical chart might display this data. Format the chart using Excel's formatting tools. Analyze the data to find the four largest clients.

4. **Open the presentation INT F-2, save it as Nomad 2, then embed a chart for each of the four largest clients in the presentation**
   Once the PowerPoint presentation is open, insert four new slides after the Primary Company Products slide, where you can embed the Excel charts. Remember, if you want to embed just the chart from an Excel worksheet that contains both data and a chart, you can copy and embed the chart alone. Now you have successfully moved data from Access to Excel, then to PowerPoint.

5. **Finish the presentation by checking for spelling errors; then set builds, transitions, slide timings, and interactive settings for the slides in your presentation**
   You may also need to enhance the presentation with objects or color, such as background shading or a template. Organize or restructure the presentation, if necessary.

6. **Save, print, then close your presentation**
   Be prepared to justify your decisions about this presentation.

FIGURE F-7: Sample Excel data

Microsoft Excel - Customer Comparison

File Edit View Insert Format Tools Data Window Help

MS Sans Serif ▼ 10 ▼ **B** *I* U ≡ ≡ ≡ 国 $ % , ⁺.₀₀ .₀₀ ⟮⟯ ⟮⟯ ⊞ ▼ ◈ ▼ A ▼

D35 ▼ =

	A	B	C	D	E
18	Product Name	All Natural Company	Product Name	CO-OP USA	
19	Herbal Blends	58,336.11	Trail Dinners	30,713.40	
20	Total	58,336.11	Total	30,713.40	
21					
22	Product Name	Chestnut Stores	Product Name	Natural Products Inc.	
23	ENergyBAR	48,873.75	ENergyBAR	120,265.00	
24	PowerUP	14,350.60	PlusBAR	57,577.08	
25	Trailaid	24,793.31	Trailaid	26,599.56	
26	Vitamix	9,066.42	Ventrix	154,925.70	
27	Total	97,084.08	Total	359,367.34	
28					
29	Product Name	Company Square	Product Name	Western Foods Inc.	
30	ENergyBAR	182,232.50	HG Original Tea	25,833.71	
31	FiberMix	26,447.05	Total	25,833.71	
32	PlusBAR	80,927.82			
33	Vitamix	17,631.90			
34	Total	307,239.27			

Cust

Ready

NUM

Start Microsoft Excel - Cus... 2:05 PM

FIGURE F-8: Sample chart

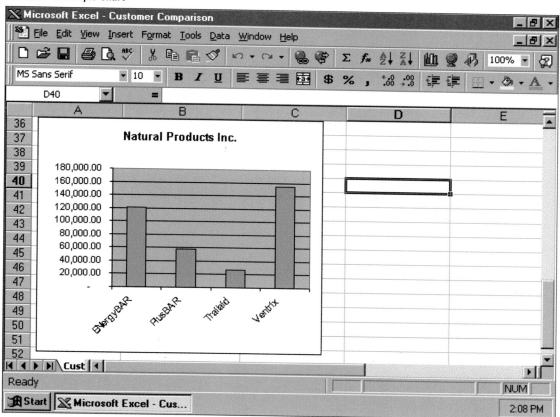

Microsoft Excel - Customer Comparison

File Edit View Insert Format Tools Data Window Help

MS Sans Serif ▼ 10 ▼ **B** *I* U ≡ ≡ ≡ 国 $ % , ⁺.₀₀ .₀₀ ⟮⟯ ⟮⟯ ⊞ ▼ ◈ ▼ A ▼

D40 ▼ =

Cust

Ready

NUM

Start Microsoft Excel - Cus... 2:08 PM

Integration

Exporting an Access Table into Word

Choosing the right Microsoft Office program for the job is an important part of creating integrated presentations. Your work will be easier and your end results more polished if you choose the right tools. ✐ Before Nomad's Board of Directors can begin negotiations to purchase H&G, Nomad's stockholders need to vote on the acquisition proposal. Chris develops a presentation describing H&G's customer and client base. To complete this presentation, he first creates a table in Word and then links it to his presentation. Chris then imports data from Excel into Microsoft Graph and embeds a chart in his presentation. He finishes by making any necessary changes to the slides.

Steps 1234

1. **Open the Access database H&G Inc.**
   You need to create a detailed list of H&G's products for the stockholder's presentation, so you decide to create a Word table from the H&G Products table.

2. **Export the H&G Products table to Word, then split the table in half and save the documents as Product table 1 and Product table 2**
   Figure F-9 shows how a published Access table appears in Word. Divide the table into two tables so they will fit on two slides in PowerPoint. Keep both documents open, and format the tables using Word's formatting features. After you publish the table to Word, close Access to free up your computer's memory.

3. **Enhance each table using Word features**
   Switch to Page Layout view and, if necessary, add the Drawing toolbar to your screen. You might want to reposition each table on the page, then add a callout explaining part of the table or add a text label that identifies the table. Also, you could add WordArt or a graphic to the table. Close Word when you are finished formatting the tables.

4. **Open the presentation INT F-3, save it as Nomad 3, then link each table you created in Word to a new slide in the presentation**
   Create two new slides before the Primary Company Products slide in the presentation, then link Product table 1 and Product table 2 to the slides. Crop and scale each of the tables to fit the slide. Depending on how you formatted the tables in Word, you may need to open the tables and edit them in Word to enhance their appearance in the presentation. Now import data from Excel into Microsoft Graph to create a chart.

5. **Open the worksheet INT F-4, save it as ENergyBAR, filter the worksheet for the ENergyBAR records, then create a new workbook with the ENergyBAR records called ENergyBAR shortlist**
   Compare your ENergyBAR shortlist worksheet to Figure F-10. You want to create a chart in PowerPoint using the client information relating to the ENergyBAR product. Close Excel and save the changes to your new worksheet, then turn off AutoFilter in the ENergyBAR workbook.

FIGURE F-9: Published Access table in a Word document

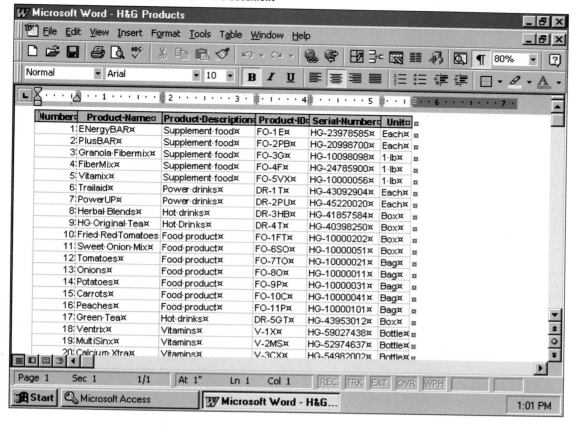

FIGURE F-10: ENergyBAR shortlist worksheet

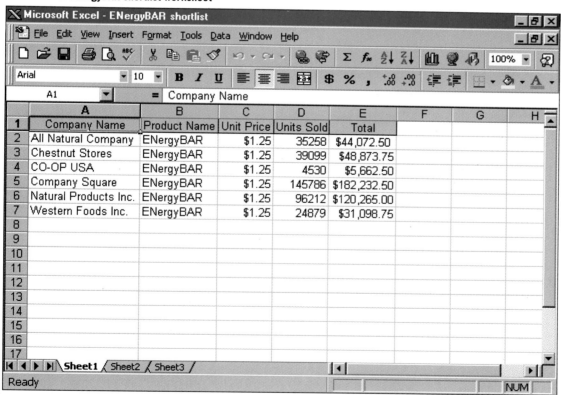

Integration

Importing Excel Data into PowerPoint

An easy way to create a chart in PowerPoint is to import existing data from Excel into PowerPoint using Microsoft Graph. Once you import data into Microsoft Graph and create a chart for your presentation, you don't need to use Excel to change or modify the chart. Chris finishes his work on this presentation by importing data from Excel into Microsoft Graph and then embedding the chart to a new slide. Chris evaluates the presentation to make sure it's organized and complete, then creates handouts in Word.

Steps

1. **Insert a new slide after the Primary Company Products slide, then create and format a Graph chart showing the ENergyBAR shortlist data**
   Use the AutoLayout button to apply the appropriate slide layout. Remember to clear the default data out of the datasheet before you import the new data from the ENergyBAR worksheet. Compare your Microsoft Graph datasheet to Figure F-11. Arrange the datasheet so the chart shows the company names, units sold, and the total. Experiment with the chart's type and 3-D view to determine the best format. Set chart options, such as chart subtype, gap depth, chart depth, gap width, and gridlines. Format the chart's data markers, data labels, and the axis. Add and format chart elements, such as a text box, an arrow, a legend, or shapes. Refer to Figure F-12 for a sample Microsoft Graph chart showing the data from the ENergyBAR shortlist worksheet. When you are finished formatting your chart, add any finishing touches to the rest of the presentation.

2. **Review the presentation, then make changes as necessary**
   You might use clipart, drawn objects, photographs, animation movies, digital movies, or sound to enhance your presentation. If necessary, change an object's appearance to better fit with the slide color scheme or slide design. Make sure the content of the presentation flows logically and is complete. You may need to add some of your own content or remove some to complete the presentation. Remember, this presentation is designed to convince the stockholders of Nomad Ltd to purchase Health & Goodness Inc.

3. **Finish the presentation by checking for spelling errors, then set builds, transitions, slide timings, and interactive settings for the presentation slides**
   To make it easy for the stockholders to follow the president as he gives the presentation, you make handouts in Word. You decide to use the Write Up feature in PowerPoint to create and link your presentation to Word because Word allows more than one slide on a handout page.

4. **Create linked handouts in Word, then save your Word document as Nomad Handouts**

5. **Save and print your presentation, then print the Word handouts**
   Be prepared to justify your presentation strategy.

FIGURE F-11: Microsoft Graph datasheet showing imported Excel data

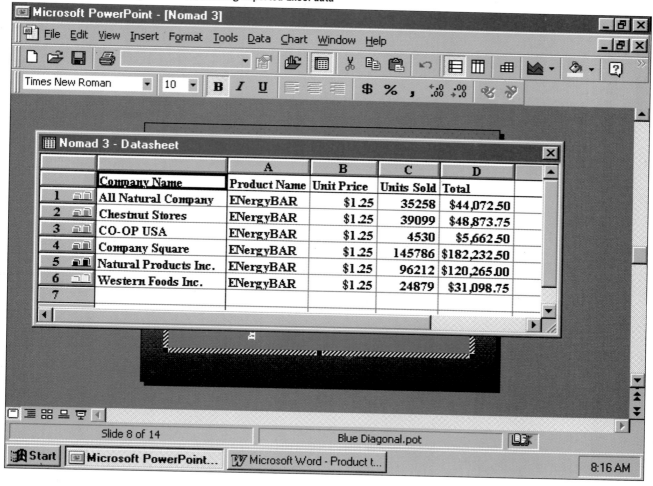

FIGURE F-12: Sample Microsoft Graph chart

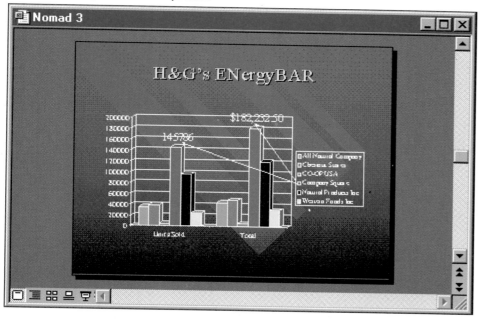

▶ Independent Challenges

1. You are a marketing analyst at Davis Press, a publishing company that produces many top-rated magazines. Recently, you were asked to research a marketing strategy for a new sports magazine that will compete with magazines such as *Sports Illustrated*. You decide to use PowerPoint to develop a presentation that you can use to illustrate your research findings and marketing recommendations.

To help you complete this independent challenge, a partially completed Word document is provided. You will complete the Word outline and then use it as the outline for a new PowerPoint presentation. Assume the following information to be true as you complete the Word outline and create a presentation:

- The name of the new magazine is *AllSports*.
- Currently, there are only three magazines that have some of the features that the new *AllSports* magazine will contain.
- *AllSports* should appeal to both men and women ages 25–55.
- *AllSports* should have articles on major field sports—for example, football, baseball, and basketball—and hobbyist sports, such as fishing and hunting.
- The magazine will focus on sports analysis and the people behind the sports.

To complete this independent challenge:

1. Open the Word document INT F-5, then save it as "AllSports Outline."
2. Review the partially completed Word document, then replace the italicized text with your own content.
3. Add information that would strengthen your presentation to the Word outline.
4. Create a new presentation using your completed Word outline. Insert the Word document into PowerPoint. Consider the results you want and how you need to adjust the text in PowerPoint.
5. Preview the presentation and plan the design of each slide. Change the slide layout, if necessary.
6. Add a template or a shaded background. Customize an existing presentation template, or create one of your own.
7. Add or create objects to enhance the slides of your presentation. Analyze each slide to see if an object can enhance the text on that slide.
8. Embed the following Word table from PowerPoint using the Insert Microsoft Word Table button:

	AllSports	*Sports Illustrated*	*Sportsman*
Type of coverage	All sport types	Major sports	Hobbyist sports
Coverage focus	Analytical, personal	Analytical	Personal
Coverage appeal	Nondiscriminatory	Male, 20s–40s	Male, 40s–60s

9. Use your own information to add one more magazine examples and two more categories to the table.
10. Format the table using Word's formatting tools, embed the table into PowerPoint, then format the table in PowerPoint.
11. Spell-check the presentation, then save it as "AllSports Magazine."
12. Set slide builds, slide timings, slide transitions, and interactive settings to all the slides.
13. Print your final presentation slides.
14. Submit the printed output and a slide show of the presentation to your instructor.

2. You are the controller for Health & Goodness Inc. (H&G), a dry foods company. In relation to the impending sale of H&G to Nomad Ltd, you must give a detailed presentation to the chief financial officer and the financial board on the revenue generated by all of H&G's clients during the last quarter. The information you give to the board will be used to help determine relevant issues regarding H&G's sale.

In this independent challenge you will analyze an Excel worksheet and then embed seven charts that you create into a PowerPoint presentation. Your presentation should be at least 10 slides long. Use the Excel worksheet provided for you to help you complete your presentation.

To complete this independent challenge:

1. Open the Excel worksheet INT F-6, then save it as "**H&G Sale**."
2. Review the partially completed Excel worksheet. You'll need to create a separate chart for each client.
3. Create an analysis of the data similar to what is shown in Figure F-13.
4. Create similar analyses of the worksheet data that enable you to design charts of each client's total product revenue, as well as the total revenue of all the clients.
5. Format each chart using Excel's formatting tools.
6. Open a new PowerPoint presentation, then save it as "H&G Financial Review."
7. You may want to use the AutoContent wizard to help with the basic content of your presentation. Consider the results you want to see in PowerPoint and how you need to design the slides of the presentation. Remember, this is primarily a financial presentation showing revenue figures from Excel.
8. Preview the presentation and plan the design of each slide. Change the slide layout, if necessary. If you used the AutoContent Wizard in Step 6, change the sample text.
9. Add a template or a shaded background, if necessary. Customize an existing presentation template, or create one of your own.
10. Switch to Excel, and embed each chart in a different slide in PowerPoint.
11. Add or create objects to enhance the slides of your presentation. Analyze each slide to see if an object can enhance the text on that slide.
12. Spell-check the presentation.
13. Set slide builds, slide timings, slide transitions, and interactive settings for all the slides.
14. Print your final presentation slides.
15. Submit the printed output and a slide show of the presentation to your instructor.

FIGURE F-13

	A	B
1	Product Name	
2	ENergyBAR	$ 432,205.00
3	FiberMix	$ 26,447.05
4	Herbal Blends	$ 58,336.11
5	HG Original Tea	$ 25,833.71
6	PlusBAR	$138,504.90
7	PowerUP	$ 14,350.60
8	Trail Dinners	$ 30,664.26
9	Trailaid	$ 51,392.87
10	Ventrix	$154,925.70
11	Vitamix	$ 26,698.32
12	Total	$ 959,358.52
13		
14		

3. Your investment group, High Rollers, has been asked to prepare a presentation based on current stock market research. To do this, you've decided to utilize the World Wide Web (WWW) and your Microsoft Office skills.

To complete this independent challenge:

1. Log on to the Internet and use your web browser to go to http://www.course.com. From there, click Student Online Companions, click the link for this textbook, then click on the Integration link for Unit F.
2. Use any of the following sites to research current investment opportunities: New York Stock Exchange, American Stock Exchange, the NASDAQ, or any other site you can find with related information.
3. Create a database called "High Rollers Data" that contains information on at least 10 stocks of interest. The stocks do not have to have the same focus (e.g., technology, medicine, or entertainment) but should include a category field that defines it. Also, include a field that contains the current cost per share.
4. Export the table to Excel, and save the workbook as "High Rollers Info."
5. Create a column that calculates the cost of 15 shares of each stock, then chart the data in this new column.
6. Create a Word outline that will be the basis for your presentation to the club and will discuss your stock recommendations. The outline should contain at least six slides. Save the outline as "High Rollers Outline."
7. Open a new PowerPoint presentation, and save it as "High Rollers Presentation."
8. Import the "High Rollers Outline" into the "High Rollers Presentation."
9. Add the Excel chart to one of the slides.
10. Set slide builds, slide timings, slide transitions, and interactive settings for all the slides.
11. Spell-check the presentation.
12. Print the slides of your final presentation.
13. Submit the printed output and a slide show of the presentation to your instructor.

Index

Index

Index

Index